BRANDS & GAMING

The computer gaming phenomenon and
its impact on brands and businesses

David Nichols
Tom Farrand
Tom Rowley
&
Matt Avery

First published 2006 by
PALGRAVE MACMILLAN
Houndmills, Basingstoke, Hampshire RG21 6XS and
175 Fifth Avenue, New York, N.Y. 10010
Companies and representatives throughout the world

PALGRAVE MACMILLAN is the global academic imprint of the Palgrave
Macmillan division of St. Martin's Press, LLC and of Palgrave Macmillan Ltd.
Macmillan® is a registered trademark in the United States, United Kingdom
and other countries. Palgrave is a registered trademark in the European Union
and other countries.

ISBN–13: 978–1–4039–9897–2
ISBN–10: 1–4039–9897–3

This book is printed on paper suitable for recycling and made from fully
managed and sustained forest sources.

A catalogue record for this book is available from the British Library.

A catalog record for this book is available from the Library of Congress.

10   9   8   7   6   5   4   3   2   1
15   14   13   12   11   10   09   08   07   06

Printed and bound in Great Britain by
Creative Print & Design (Wales) Ebbw Vale

Contents

Figures and tables

Acknowledgments

To Lara without whom none of this
would have been possible.

CHAPTER 1

Are you ready to play?

The global gaming phenomenon

Saturday night, KL

It's a clammy Saturday night in downtown Kuala Lumpur and you're looking for the action. You walk past a strip-lit bar where couples are sharing a few sad beers. Uh-huh. Then a restaurant or two, full of overdressed suburban hicks and their extended families. No way. The next street looks more promising, but the bouncers outside the clubs look more likely to drag you in than turn you away. Then you notice a steady drift of people towards a mall on the road to the Chinese market. And something tells you that not all of these folks are late night shoppers.

Six floors of Asian retail beckon as the teeming escalator swallows you up and disgorges you at level three. You push past stalls dangling mobile phones like salami in an Italian deli, whose proprietors can banter with six or seven customers all at the same time. On you go, past tiny bench–chair–lamp outlets where men with tiny screw-drivers and soldering irons are fiddling with circuit boards and sim cards, hot-wiring phones and PDAs (personal digital assistants).

The frenetic commerce is starting to make you feel dizzy, but it's nothing compared to the clamor and fervor of what comes next: the gaming area. There is no formal entrance; you simply stumble into a space filled with line after line of hulking machines, blinking and throbbing to the commands of swarms of young people. Most of the din is being generated by the shooting games, where teenagers holding futuristic guns are picking off lolloping video apparitions with a practiced ease suggesting hours, maybe weeks, of practice. On closer inspection, you notice that each shooter is assisted by a friend, calmly pointing out the next target. There's plenty of teamwork here. These are not sorry, anti-social loners; these are clearly hip young people having a great night out with their friends.

Push on over to the second line of machines and there's an altogether different experience. These are the dancing games: lines of one-meter-square, multi-colored, *Saturday Night Fever*-style dance floors, attached to speakers pumping out disco music. In front of each one is a screen covered in wild hieroglyphics that tell the player the pattern to follow with his feet. You might ask what would possess a 20-year-old guy in designer shirt and shades to prance about doing bad disco dancing on a machine, in full view of his mates and groups of girls? The answer is simply that nobody here is compromising their cool. This is normal behavior – a hugely social pastime, with friends comparing moves, grooving to the music, gyrating to the beat of the gaudy arcade box.

A further sweep of the area takes you past flight simulators jolting around on their pistons, shaking the fillings out of their pilots' teeth. There are also racing games aplenty: yards of Recaro seats stretched out into the darkness, propelling eager teams around Daytona, NASCAR tracks, and strange dystopian cities set up for joy-riding alone.

But all that is only the warm-up. Because the real action is taking place further on. Beyond the ranks of gaming machines you find the real cutting edge of the modern entertainment industry – the LAN arena. This huge, dimly lit cavern is filled with more than a thousand PCs, each with a trendily-dressed young gamer, all with headphones clamped to their heads, hunched over keyboard and mouse, frantically clicking and tapping. Some have small groups of friends behind them, egging them on; others are playing solo. As you saunter past, you can glimpse the whirling, spitting, flaring action that has them glued to the screens in front of them. What is happening here is not immediately obvious to the uninitiated. It might appear that these gamers are wrapped up in their own little fantasy worlds, oblivious to everyone around them. In fact, they're not. Most of them are playing games as part of teams composed of several others in the room. The LAN – or local area network – means that all the computers you see are linked together. Gamers pitch up, pay an hourly fee, then hit a computer and choose a game they want to play. They might decide to become an engineer in a team of World War II special forces attempting to take a

German machinegun post. They might be racing against each other in *ToCA*, a touring car game. Perhaps as many as a hundred people are blasting away at each other in *Counter-Strike* – a type of game known as a "first-person shooter" (FPS). And another 200 or more people in the arena might start roaming the Nek Forest or the Thundering Steppes in the company of a band of extraordinary creatures (each representing another player in the room) as they explore *EverQuest II*'s fantasy world of Norrath – in the company of a further 100,000 gamers across the globe. In fact, there are a great many games being played back and forth across the network all at the same time, each with its own rhythm of triumph and defeat, exhilaration and disappointment. One moment, a cluster of people in one corner will cheer and punch the air to celebrate a victory; others will kick their chairs back from the screen and slap their desks in disgust. Wherever you look, there are high fives and backslapping, new friendships being formed, chat-up lines being tested, and old acquaintances being renewed.

In KL this evening, this is where it's at. If you're looking to hang out with old buddies, or go somewhere to make new friends, if you're seeking thrills and action, if you want a challenge, if you want to find out how you stack up against your peers, then the LAN arena is the place to be. The bars, the clubs, the music venues, and multiplexes are for yesterday's boys and girls. Here you can almost taste the adrenaline in the air. This is where it's happening all right.

But despite all the cheers and flashing lights, the slogans and explosions, there is one key feature of the modern world that is missing from both the LAN arena and the gaming area. There are no brands here. For a marketeer it is an extraordinary experience. You are standing in the middle of hordes of affluent but hard-to-reach young consumers and you are surrounded by hi-tech media spaces on every side and yet there is not a brand name to be seen. ... No, that's not quite true. There is one: a Ferrari-branded, Italian street-driving game. So what is this? A questionable brand extension perhaps? Or a smart seeding strategy that is targeting tomorrow's billionaire bankers? The apparent total lack of communications strategy makes it very hard to tell.

Scenes like this one in KL are repeated right across Asia – from Chiang Mai to Shanghai, from Pusan to Kyoto – on any night of the week. But this is not simply an Asian phenomenon. It is just the most public manifestation of a mega-trend that is sweeping the entire world: the swift and irresistible rise of gaming at the very heart of global entertainment culture.

The gaming phenomenon

In many countries, newspapers have been happy to dismiss gaming as nothing more than a teenage fad, the preserve of solitary pubescent boys with stay-at-home acne and twitchy thumbs. But gaming today is about far more than teens and arcades and *Pacman* and *Pong*. Gaming means a silver fox in Fort Worth playing Microsoft *Combat Flight Simulator* online against a young engineering undergrad in Kathmandu. It's a sultry Parisian receptionist whiling away a quiet ten minutes playing a game of *Hearts* against her counterparts in Brisbane, Frankfurt, Shanghai, and Cape Town. It's a stressed-out executive pummeling his PSP (PlayStation Portable) on the bullet train out of Tokyo late on Friday night. It's dedicated cyber athletes competing for million-dollar prize money in global tournaments, or representing their country against the hottest talent from 70 other nations at the World Cyber Games. Because, while much of the media held its nose and looked away, gamers have been quietly creating a whole new industry on a massive global scale.

We have come to expect that the next "Big Thing" will always be announced in the manner of the Apocalypse, with fanfares and fly-pasts, skydivers, soccer stars, and celebrities in stretches. But video and computer gaming has never indulged itself in the kind of high-kicking razzle-dazzle so beloved of the music and film industries. Instead, it has crept up on everyone as insidiously as a high tide edging its way up the embankment of a river. The column inches in the press might have grown slightly over the past few years and months, but this bears no relation to the phenomenon they are reporting. Because although the gaming tide has yet to burst its banks, it has already flooded the basements of our culture and is now seeping deep into the fabric of our social life.

CEO TEASER

Which is bigger – the music, film, or computer gaming industries?

So exactly how big is computer and video gaming? As big as the $10 billion film industry? Think bigger. The $15 billion music industry? Bigger still. The $20 billion home video industry? Even bigger than that. With a market value of over $25 billion, gaming now outstrips the lot of them. According to analysts at PricewaterhouseCoopers, worldwide game industry revenue is set to rocket to $54.6 billion in 2009.

Let's repeat that. Gaming is now bigger than music, film, and video. Kidman and Cruise? Jagger and Richards? These guys are midgets when you set them next to Lara Croft and *The Sims*. When *Halo 2* was launched in November 2004, it took over $100 million on its first day of release. The stunning success of this first-person shooter that runs on Microsoft's Xbox prompted Bill Gates to boast that it was:

> *"an opening day that's greater than any motion picture has ever had in history."*

And he had a point. At the time the record box office take for a movie on its opening day was "just" $40.4 million, achieved by *Spider-Man 2*.

What's more, since the turn of the millennium, computer gaming has been enjoying double-digit growth at the global level, becoming a

Figure 1.1

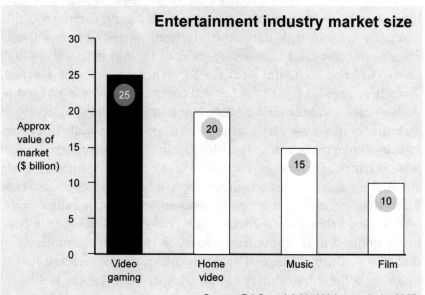

Source: B.I.G. and Added Value analysis, 2005

true mass market mainstream business; while in the same period, the film and music industries have been in decline or, at best, stagnant. Indeed, as gaming commands an increasing share of the entertainment market, it is helping to drive the move away from TV as well, especially among younger people. At the same time, the growth of new channels, especially recent developments in online gaming, has helped to create completely new social structures and cultural icons. It seems likely that, in the not too distant future, gamers, game characters, and game developers will be acknowledged as the new film stars, directors, and power players in the global entertainment industry.

Statistics struggle to capture a sea change such as this. Our research suggests that in some parts of Europe as many as 83 percent of people play some form of computer or video game two or three times a week. If that is indeed the case, it would put gaming on a par with eating, drinking, and watching TV as *the* human activities of choice ... 83 percent? It sounds preposterous, doesn't it?

But take a quick look at the businesses behind gaming and things start to add up. Look at Sony. Everyone remembers them as the guys who coined it on the Walkman. And since then, of course, they've added digital cameras, flat screen TVs, mobile phones, MP3 players and God knows what else to their portfolio. But do you know what their biggest seller is today? It's PlayStation. And it's not just their biggest seller; it happens to be bigger than all the divisions of the company combined. What about Electronic Arts? Heard of them? They're not just the publisher of some of the top games titles, like *Medal of Honor, FIFA,* and *Need For Speed*; according to the *Financial Times* they are also one of the top 400 companies in the world today, with a market value of $16 billion. Not bad for a young company in an industry of whose very existence most people are quite unaware.

The strange thing is how few other businesses have cottoned on to what is happening here. Perhaps even more staggering than the sheer size of the gaming industry is the extent to which its potential as a new marketing and advertising space has been ignored. A handful of the world's top brands – like McDonald's, Nike, and Intel – have been brave enough to fiddle with the joystick (somewhat tentatively, it must be said), but the vast majority of brand owners are totally unaware of the extraordinary opportunity that is just about to slip out of their grasp.

Table 1.1

The *Financial Times* Global Top 500, 2005			
Rank	Company	Market value ($m)	Turnover ($m)
145	Sony	36,986.6	69,941.7
383	Electronic Arts	15,944.9	2,957.1

The scale of the opportunity

To get an idea of the scale of this opportunity, think back to a warm New York night 60-odd years ago. On the evening of 1 July 1941, a few tech-savvy baseball fans would have been sitting round their new-fangled TV sets watching the Dodgers take on the Philadelphia Phillies, when the broadcast was interrupted by the face of a black Bulova watch. Its second hand ticked through a full minute and then it disappeared and the baseball resumed. Most of the audience probably didn't realize what the hell was going on, but they had in fact just witnessed the first ever TV commercial. It was the start of an era of unprecedented success for those brands that saw the potential of this new medium and seized the day. Think of P&G and Unilever, think of Coke and Pepsi; in fact, think of any household name. It was TV advertising that propelled brands like these into a position of marketing gods to three generations of consumers, brands that reigned supreme for over 60 years. Those brands that didn't spot what TV could do are, of course, long gone – forgotten footnotes in the unread tome of business history.

It is not fanciful to suggest that today we are at a similar tipping point for the communications industry. Any advertiser will tell you that the days of the 30-second TV spot are numbered – its ability to deliver mass audiences shattered by channel proliferation and its very existence threatened by the rise of the cursed personal video recorder (PVR), which allows ever increasing numbers of viewers to skip the ad breaks altogether. But gaming has the ability to deliver huge audiences on a global scale – and we are certainly not just talking teens here, either. Look at the ownership profile of the Sony PlayStation 2, the most popular gaming console. You might assume that this would be heavily skewed to teenagers, but not a bit of it. With the console retailing at around $300 to $400 for most of its time in stores and games costing around $50 a title, these are not things that ordinary teenagers can pick up with their pocket money; they would have to be significant parental purchases. Indeed, the figures show that 29.2 percent of PlayStation 2s are used by the 24–34 age group and there is even a significant proportion in the 35+ age bracket. That means half of the user base of the world's most popular games-dedicated console is made up of people over 24 years old. Add to that the fact that female gamers, traditionally accounting for just a fraction of the gaming population, now make up one of the fastest growing audiences in the category and you have a truly powerful, far-reaching new media channel whose potential it is sheer folly to ignore.

The rules for this new space are quite unlike any that the communications industry has ever played by before. For sure, gamers represent a significant new group of consumers for businesses to target, and there are many exciting new opportunities opening up for brands of

Figure 1.2

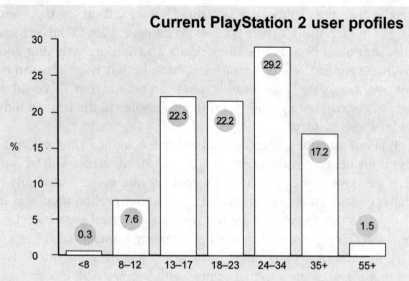

Source: Datamonitor UK

all types to offer lifestyle products, food, drink, and much more besides. But it needs to be remembered that this audience is extremely switched-on, media-literate, and highly cynical about conventional marketing ploys. Gamers are, by their very nature, proactive and will not be led by the nose like their passive, TV-viewing parents and grandparents. It would be a big mistake to assume that reaching out to these people and persuading them to accept branding as part of the scenery of their virtual worlds will be easy.

Conclusion

As gaming moves further into the mainstream, its influence will start to ripple out into many other areas. At the most straightforward level, we will see the growing importance of media that specifically target gamers: magazines, websites, TV programs, many of which will seem alien in content, style, and codes to conventional marketeers and brand owners. We will also see gaming sections appearing in lifestyle magazines and popular newspapers; the UK's leading tabloid, *The Sun*, is already running a gaming column as a way of making the paper relevant to younger readers.

And, at a more general level, we should also notice a subtle but inexorable shift in the balance of cultural power in the world. As new creative centers for global entertainment develop, the supremacy of the USA (and Hollywood in particular) in the entertainment industry seems bound to decline. Asia is already leading the way in terms of numbers of gamers, but at the moment most games are created in the West and then played globally; this situation may well change as Asia becomes more influential. The precise ramifications of all this are still unclear, but new roles in the entertainment industry will mean that brands looking to leverage entertainment properties will have to deal with new power brokers, new channels, and new approaches. While this may prove problematic for some traditional brands, it opens up significant opportunities for new non-established brands to get into the big time. One thing is certain, though: the gaming phenomenon is something that no brand owner, marketeer, or advertiser can afford to ignore for a moment longer.

So do you accept the challenge? Are you ready to play?

Frankly, you don't have a choice.

SIMS SO REAL

THE SIMS 2: NIGHTLIFE   12+

PUBLISHER: Electronic Arts
FORMATS: PC
PRICE: £19.99
WHAT'S THE STORY? Get the party started with this second expansion pack for the hit Sims 2 game. Dating, clubbing, karaoke and a meal for two are all on the menu.
HOW DOES IT HANDLE? Gameplay remains pretty much the same as in previous versions, plus an enjoyment meter shows how much fun you've given your characters.
SCREEN GRAB OR SCREEN DRAB? The nightclubs and bars you make look great.
HOW LONG TILL I'M BORED? Nightlife is a lot more exciting than the University add-on. Addictive.
VERDICT: 84%

MIDNIGHT CLUB 3: DUB EDITION

OUT: Now. **RATING:** 12+. **FORMATS:** PSP. **PUBLISHER:** Rockstar Games. **PRICE:** £34.99.
THIS ace console racer has been shrunk for the Sony handheld – but ends up in the slow lane while the competition roars past.

It does deliver some exciting open-city racing but in portable form it doesn't work as well as on your home machine.

The main issue is that it's slower to load – always a downside for games you're trying to play on the move.

It's not a total disappointment, though – blinging up your motor still works well. But as an overall port from a very impressive title, it seems to have run out of fuel.

VERDICT: 74%

TOTAL OVERDOSE

OUT: Now. **RATING:** 18. **FORMATS:** PS2, Xbox, PC. **PUBLISHER:** Eidos. **PRICE:** £29.99-£39.99.
GET your trigger finger ready to combat a Mexican crimewave.

Set in 1989, the game stars you as Ramiro Cruz, an undercover agent desperate to avenge his father's death and brother's injury while working for the government against drug cartels.

Packed full of atmosphere, it has a really enjoyable story that's brought to life with superb detail and backgrounds.

The gameplay is exciting in parts but it's nothing new and doesn't always fulfil its promise.

The driving, bad guys and tequila are quite cool – just not red hot.

VERDICT: 72%

The popular media around the world are now featuring gaming on a regular basis – as in this column from *The Sun*

CHAPTER 2

Scoping the map

Gaming today

Battling clans

Watching the giant screen at the IMAX cinema at the London Science Museum feels like gazing through the transparent side of a spaceship onto a parallel universe. The setting on the screen is somehow earthly, with recognizably human figures in World War II vintage uniforms making their way through a war-blasted landscape, but the sheer scale and intensity and vibrancy of the action is definitely out of this world.

As the audience watches, two professional American pundits are rattling through a commentary at a pace fit for a cattle auction. And they need to, just to keep up with what's happening. The action that fizzes and explodes across the giant screen whirls in a paradiddle of action, faster than the quickest karate move you've ever seen, more sudden than the most lethal fencing strike ...

Beneath the huge screen, two teams – or "clans" – are hunkered down in front of a bank of PCs, linked by a state-of-the-art local area network (LAN). From the back of their tops you can read that they're called the 4 Kings and the Lemmings. These young men and women are cyber athletes of the first order. As they rock back and forth over their mice and keyboards, they bark coded instructions to other clan members over their wrap-around microphones. It soon becomes apparent that each of them is represented by a presence on the giant screen. Their ability to memorize three-dimensional space is uncanny as they navigate their game characters through a maze of staircases and corridors. They have the reflexes of a top goalkeeper – able to spot and respond to a threat before anyone in the audience has even registered the enemy presence. And as their game characters crouch and spin and fire and reload, the gamers' fingers blur on their keyboards like pianists performing a Chopin allegretto ...

But just in case you're thinking – Hang on a moment, what the hell is going on here? – let's pause the action and fill in a bit of background. What we are witnessing is the leading edge of hardcore gaming: a Masters gaming tournament for some of the world's top professional clans, sponsored by computer giant Intel and offering serious cash prizes. And, no, this is not a futuristic fantasy; this was an event that we were lucky enough to get tickets for way back in December 2002. And you heard that right: top venue, professional teams, corporate sponsorship. Nor was this some kind of strange one-off. Indeed over the past few years an international circus of professional gaming tournaments like this one has developed around the world, the most prestigious being the World Cyber Games, an annual event that has been held in Seoul, San Francisco, and Singapore with 800 plus participants from over 70 countries competing to be hailed as the best in the world. Professional gaming is now being taken so seriously that we have even seen the world's first checkbook player transfer, with Norwegian *Counter-Strike* player, 17-year-old Ola "ElemeNt" Moum, moving from the world champion Swedish clan Schroet Kommando to the US-based NoA for an undisclosed fee. How long will it be before stars of the gaming scene start to have their own agents?

The game being played on the IMAX screen at the Science Museum was *Return To Castle Wolfenstein* – a type of game known as a "first-person shooter," in which the players are separate characters who control their view of the environment, as they shoot enemies with a variety of weaponry. (In this case, the clans were using a multi-player version of the game for two teams.) The game is set during World War II and involves teams of Axis versus Allies who battle for control of Nazi war secrets or vital strategic installations in an attempt to determine the course of history. To the spectators in the cinema (many of whom will never have played a game like this

before), the on-screen action looks like an exciting cross between witnessing a fast-and-furious team sport – think soccer, basketball, or ice hockey – and watching a movie.

However, many of the audience will have a particular appreciation of the skill of the clans involved because it's a game they will have played themselves. Published by Activision, the online version of the game gives players the chance to form a team with other gamers across the globe to achieve their mission objectives. So, if you have a copy of *Return To Castle Wolfenstein* installed on your computer, it's possible to come home from work, grab a beer from the fridge, go online, and storm a machinegun post in company with players from Seoul, Baltimore, Perth, and Honolulu who are playing, like you, in real time on their own computer screens back home. Each member of the team will have a different role: there'll be engineers with the power to blast breaches in walls, a lieutenant who can call in air strikes, as well as snipers, machinegunners, and flame throwers. Should you find yourself struck down by enemy fire, you may well be attended by a medic who suddenly appears beside you. The medic, of course, will be another player in the game, just like you, with his or her own job, own life, own identity, somewhere else far away in the real world, but right next to you in the virtual one.

Online gaming is still a relatively new phenomenon, but, powered by the spread of fast broadband connections, it is one that is growing rapidly. So, if you're a *Star Wars* fan, you can buy the *Star Wars Galaxies* game, go online, and enter an entire universe based on your favorite movies, which has been created in cyberspace. As you wander around, you can meet other characters (controlled by people somewhere else in the world) and interact with them, for example, by inviting them to join you on a perilous quest, or even challenging them to a duel. Equally, car racing fans can now buy a racing game such as the *Forza Motorsport* game, customize a virtual car to their own specifications and then go online and race it against other people from the far side of the planet.

We suspect that games similar to these are destined to become the mainstay of the gaming industry, especially with the advent of a new generation of games known as massively multi-player online first-person shooters (MMOFPS) and massively multi-player online role-playing games (MMORPG) – of which more later in the book –

but at the time of writing they are still very much at the leading edge of its evolution. In some parts of the world, like South Korea, such games are now the norm, but in most places mainstream gaming lags some way behind. So, let's return from the future for a few moments and take stock of what's going on in the industry's mainstream right now, by looking around an imaginary games retailer in a typical shopping mall or high street.

Gaming platforms

On walking into the store, it should be immediately apparent that it is divided between the major gaming platforms: in other words, the machines on which people play their games. The first key distinction here is between the PC – the catch-all platform – and the consoles. One of the big advantages of the PC is that it is rarely purchased exclusively for gaming so, from the gamer's point of view, the purchase price of this kind of platform is often invisible. PC gaming has also enjoyed a significant head-start in the hugely popular – and rapidly growing – world of networked gaming. The exponential growth of online multi-player gaming can be attributed to two key factors – the processor speed of today's average home PC and the rapid roll-out – and uptake – of broadband. PCs also offer the possibility of upgrading components (particularly graphics cards), which allows developers to design ever more sophisticated games, while the computer's ability to perform complex calculations on the fly has given rise to a raft of games (such as real-time strategy [RTS]), that depend on high-end processing power. However, PCs do require some technological savvy and, for many people, using one will always be far more bound up with work than with leisure.

Consoles, on the other hand, are nearly always associated with entertainment. The use of the game pad and other peripherals such as joysticks and steering wheels provides an intense gaming experience, while their multi-player option allows friends to game together. They are also easy to use, as they are geared solely to gaming and come with plug-and-play capabilities.

Those who opt for consoles will find that there are three obvious options. Sony have enjoyed the lead market position for the past ten years with their highly successful PlayStation platforms.

PlayStation 3

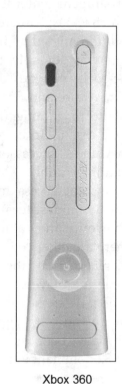

Xbox 360

Nintendo Revolution

2006 line-up of top gaming consoles

Launched in 1995, the original PlayStation was succeeded by the PlayStation 2 in 2000, confirming its premier position – which looks likely to be consolidated when the next-generation PlayStation 3 is launched in 2006.

Next in the pecking order (and closing the gap) is the new kid on the block: Microsoft. Banking on superior technology and networked connectivity, the high-tech giant has leapfrogged more established players with its Xbox platform. Designed to be located in the living room, not the bedroom, the sleek black box signaled Microsoft's intent to establish a foothold as *the* entertainment portal for the home. This is set to continue with the launch of the sleek silver Xbox 360, placing itself ever more powerfully as the entertainment center in the home.

Which leaves Nintendo. Their popular platform, the GameCube, was differentiated by its bold colors and cutesy design, indicating that it was squarely targeted at the younger gamer. This was reflected by the raft of popular cartoon-like characters such as Mario, Wario, and Sonic, who all inhabit the Technicolor worlds of platform gaming (now fully 3D). Nintendo are now trying to leverage their huge and much-loved back catalog through GameCube's successor, Revolution, which is fully backwards compatible (unlike Xbox 360). Revolution owners will therefore have instant access to thousands of games, downloadable for relatively modest fees – a smart move for a third player focusing on the youth and value end of the market.

There are other consoles, such as Phantom and Gizmondo, but a quick glance round the store should tell you that these are clearly not big volume players, an impression which our research certainly supports. We spoke to over 1000 consumers aged 15–54 in the UK and Germany and, as Figure 2.1 shows PC/Mac-based games are narrowly edged into second place by console games, with PlayStation and PS2 dominant in that area.

The reasons for choosing one console over another may include factors like price, peer pressure, technical superiority, and – critically – which games are available for that particular platform. Most of the new generation of consoles will be optimized for instant out-of-box broadband connection, allowing gamers to play online directly from the console itself.

Game titles

Once you have made your choice of platform, then it's down to the games themselves. There are a huge number of different types of games serving all manner of interests and occasions. To pick some at random: you might choose one for the kids – the incredibly successful *Sims 2*, perhaps, in which they can invent and control a virtual family as it interacts with others in their neighborhood. Or you might seek a few thrills yourself with *Combat Flight Simulator*, so realistic that it comes close to the simulators that are used to

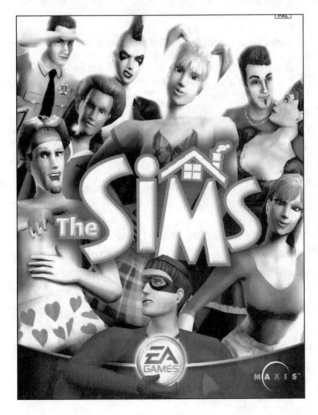

**A typical choice
of big name
titles from your
local computer
games store**

Figure 2.1

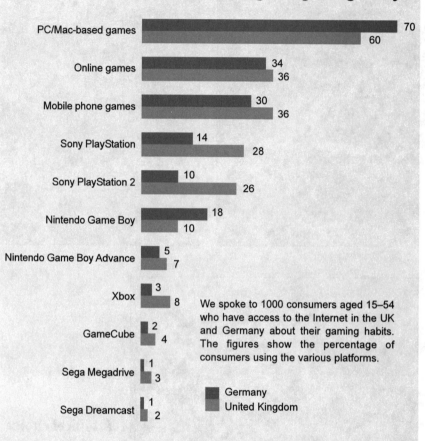

train pilots in the world's air forces. Or, if you're feeling business-minded, why not go for *RollerCoaster Tycoon*, a complex strategy game where you build and operate a theme park for maximum profit? You will also probably find a few "platform games" (not to be confused with gaming platforms!) like *Mario*, *Sonic the Hedgehog*, *Psychonauts*, and *Rayman: Hoodlum's Revenge*. This is one of the oldest gaming genres, originating in arcade games and featuring cartoon-style characters which gamers control in a variety of locations, as they try to avoid environmental traps while

Figure 2.2

Gaming styles and genres

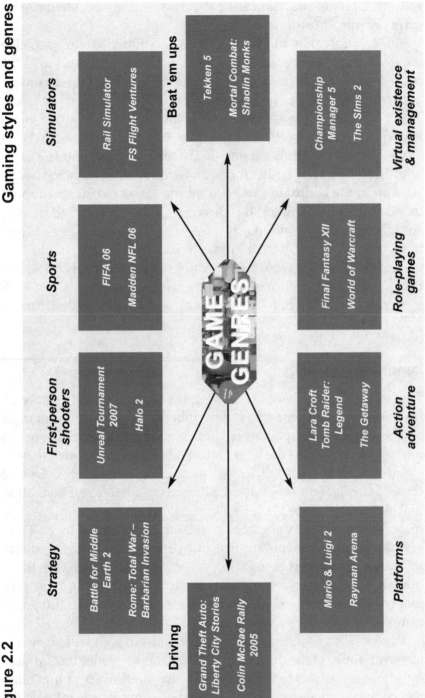

collecting points and "power-ups" (objects giving the character an extra one-off, short-term ability).

But certainly not all these games are for kids. In fact, like movies, many games are so adult that they come with an "18" sticker on the front. In *Playboy: The Mansion*, you get the chance to play the character of Hef and pursue the Playboy lifestyle. *Grand Theft Auto: San Andreas* takes a no-holds-barred look at gangland America, while *Singles*, a title from German publishers Deep Silver, is a sort of adult version of *The Sims* (though nothing to do with EA's family-friendly title) allowing you to see what really goes on in the bedrooms and behind the shower curtains of those innocent-looking families. Besides these, you will also find driving simulations, beat 'em ups, third-person adventure games, and many, many other different kinds. To catalog them all would be a Herculean task that would fill most of the pages of this book, but if you want more information on the different genres, along with examples and notes of the style, flavor, and appeal of each, turn to Appendix 1 on page 127.

Peripherals

The other part of the game store's shelf space will probably be taken up by a fearsome array of peripherals. The functions of most of these are self-explanatory (force-feedback joysticks, special mice, keyboards, and the like), but a few of them may catch the eye as offering new possibilities for interacting with games. One of these is the *EyeToy*, which is a USB camera linked to a PlayStation that sits on top of the player's TV and detects the movements they make in response to the game on the screen in front of them. Players can perform a whole range of activities like copying dance moves on the screen or fighting off attackers or saving footballs that appear to be flying towards them. The game can then give players marks for their performance – or they can take turns and compete against each other.

Anyone with a teenage daughter (or, indeed, son) will be aware, however dimly, of the dance mat phenomenon. A dance mat is made up of nine pressure-sensitive squares that are linked to a gaming device that displays moves on the screen. The dancer follows the

18-certificate games

patterns with her (or his) feet and so learns routines for all the latest chart hits, which are, of course, regularly updated.

You may also come across a special type of board fitted with motion sensors that is used for snowboarding and skateboarding

EyeToy Play, and Sony's innovative
EyeToy camera (bottom left)

Formula 1-style driving cockpit

games. Players stand on the board and move around in response to the terrain that they see on the screen in front of them. The sensors accurately register the shifting weight on the board which, in turn, affects the scene displayed on the screen. The experience is so realistic that it is now often used as a cheap and effective form of training for the real thing, to improve skills and learn new tricks.

You can also buy reasonably cheaply a force-feedback steering wheel for your favorite driving games, or for the complete experience why not buy a collapsible Formula 1 cockpit with ground-scraping seat, steering wheel, and pedals?

The desire for more realistic and immersive gaming experiences means that peripherals like these are only the tip of the iceberg, with ever more extraordinary gadgets hitting the market every month.

Mobile gaming

One of the most important and fastest growing areas is mobile gaming. This term is used fairly loosely to cover gaming on mobile phones as well as gaming on handheld devices such as the PlayStation Portable, the Nintendo Game Boy, and its spiritual successor the DS. These handhelds have proved phenomenally popular. In fact, Sony was obliged to delay the European launch of the PSP in order to cope with the overwhelming demand in its original launch markets of Japan and the USA.

However, it needs to be emphasized that mobile phones and handhelds meet very different needs. The performance of a PlayStation Portable, for example, is to all intents and purposes as good as the PlayStation 2, allowing users to play all their regular games while on the move. Mobile phones, on the other hand, offer something completely different. Their technical limitations mean that they provide a far less satisfying gaming experience; some might even describe it as "dumbed down." However, because mobiles are always with us, they are an ideal way of delivering games that kill time and relieve boredom and, indeed, gaming is now a key part of the main mobile operators' offer. It is also true to say that things have moved on from the days of *Snake*, with big improvements in mobile phone games' graphics and the complexity of game mechanics, and there are now a variety of downloadable titles for mobile phones, ranging from classic puzzle games to cut-down versions of the latest PC and console titles such as *Star Wars Episode III* and *AMF Xtreme Bowling*. As take-up of 3G phones grows and mobiles increasingly converge with other devices, there would appear to be considerable potential in this area – which, again, we'll pick up on in Chapter 6.

Gambling

None of the kinds of gaming mentioned so far in this chapter have any element of gambling in them. However, that does not mean gambling has no part to play in the development of gaming. Casino sites offering games such as poker and blackjack online have proved to be enormous money-spinners. In fact, when PartyGaming, the company behind the UK's successful Party Poker website, decided to seek a listing on the London stock exchange in mid-2005, the company's value was initially estimated at around £5 billion – bigger than British Airways and EMI combined. Not bad for a company that hardly existed just four years previously!

Conclusion

Certainly, the choice of both games and the platforms on which to play them is bewilderingly large, appealing to wildly different tastes and interests. People may come to gaming seeking a whole range of different things: a mental challenge perhaps, or thrills, or mastery of a certain skill, or direct competition with others, to name just a few. From the marketeer's point of view, there is clearly potential for segmenting consumers according to the game they are playing, not just in terms of the kind of person they are and their aspirations and motivations, but also according to the mood they are likely to be in, and even the times of day at which they are likely to play a given game. This could have significant implications for any business trying to find new and better ways to target potential customers. So next, let's take a look at some of the ways that are being developed to leverage the potential of gaming – the weapons currently available for brand owners, marketeers, and advertisers to deploy.

CHAPTER 3

Target identified ... deploy weapons

Brands in the gaming arena

Put yourself in the position of a marketeer when TV was in its infancy. How would you have set about tapping into the power of this unprecedented new medium? Perhaps you could pay TV manufacturers to plaster your logo on the fascia around the screen itself. That would certainly guarantee you a fair amount of eyeball time. Or you could publish photographs in magazines of people enjoying your products while watching this glamorous new invention. You could even market new product lines for viewers to wear, use, or consume as they watched their favorite program: TV slippers, TV chairs, TV drinks, or TV dinners. Or would you try to get inside the box somehow? Why not have your logo flickering away in the top corner of the screen all the time? Or perhaps you could get your brands to appear within the programs like they did in the old radio soap operas. Or how about using the gaps between the programs? ... Hmmm ...

With the benefit of hindsight, the solution seems laughably obvious, but 60 years ago any of those options – and many more – might have been perfectly plausible. Today, gaming presents us with a similar conundrum. We might be able to identify our target, but which weapons to deploy to attack it is far from clear. So let's look at seven of the ways in which marketeers are seeking to unlock the commercial potential of this extraordinary new medium.

The gaming celebrity

Probably the outstanding early example of the commercial exploitation of gaming by a major brand is the case of Lara Croft: the first real gaming icon and still the biggest star the industry has spawned to date. Lara was created by the young video artist Toby Gard in the studios of Core Design in the English Midlands town of Derby in 1995 and made her debut in the first *Tomb Raider* game the following year. In the game, Lara is hired to track down three parts of a mysterious artifact called the Atlantean Scion – a mission which takes her through Peru, Egypt, Rome, and the lost city of Atlantis. Along the way she has to negotiate a fearsome array of sadistic booby-traps as well as shooting her way out of tangles with hostile wildlife, such as rats, tigers, and even a Tyrannosaurus rex.

1996 – *Tomb Raider*   2003 – *Tomb Raider:*   2006 – *Tomb Raider:*
The Angel of Darkness   *Legend*

The evolution of Lara Croft

Although it was still fairly early days for the gaming industry, *Tomb Raider* rapidly became a global phenomenon. Within just a couple of years, the figure of a busty young woman wearing shorts and holding a pair of guns became instantly recognizable, not just within the gaming world but by many outside it as well. The communications industry was perhaps slow to spot Lara Croft's potential. After all, here was an icon not only immediately recognizable in her home territory (the UK), but with a rapidly growing audience all around the rest of the world. At the time, brands were desperate for more stars like David Beckham who could break out of narrow interest groups and reach across national boundaries, so surely Lara's appeal should have been obvious. Perhaps it was simply that she wasn't flesh-and-blood. Because, although there were many examples of cartoon characters achieving international acclaim (just think Mickey Mouse), there was no precedent for a digitally-generated superstar emerging from a computer game. Lara was undeniably famous, but somehow she wasn't seen as a "celebrity."

All that was to change in 1999, when she took her first swig of a traditional British beverage called Lucozade. This sweet, fizzy, orange drink had been a part of British life for three-quarters of a century, but for much of its existence it had been seen as a health tonic (often sold by pharmacies) to boost energy or help people recuperating from illness. However, in the early 1990s, Lucozade successfully re-invented itself as a sports energy drink, and by the end of the decade it was looking to step into the mainstream and become a brand that would be sold out of the same fridges as Coke and Pepsi.

Lucozade wanted to make the drink more relevant and attractive to the core 18 to 24-year-old male and female market, and its visionary idea was to build a campaign around nothing more than a bunch of digits – a.k.a. Lara Croft. Although gaming was an important activity of consumers in the target group, this certainly didn't mean that it was to be aimed exclusively at gamers. For this reason, it was made clear that this would not be treated as a Lucozade–*Tomb Raider* tie-up, but more as a celebrity endorsement. However, for this to work effectively, it was absolutely crucial that brand and character shared core values. From Lucozade's point of view, unless Lara could capture the essential personality of the brand, their money would be wasted; while from the point of view of the game's publisher, Eidos, if gamers rejected the ads, it could seriously compromise *Tomb Raider*'s credibility.

As it turned out, the fit between Lara and Lucozade was perfect. Lara was a bullet-proof personality; she wouldn't get messily divorced or age or experiment with recreational drugs. It was also easy to imagine the hyperactive heroine refueling with a high energy drink – and when the TV spots were activated, that's exactly what they showed her doing. In one of them, she was trying to escape from a pack of savage monster-hounds when she came to a yawning chasm; quickly, she gulped down some Lucozade which gave her the energy to leap to safety on the other side of the drop. Another showed her stopping for a friendly drink of Lucozade with her enemies while the player of the game had paused to get a drink. This cleverly highlighted not only Lucozade's fit with gaming, but also the fact that gaming had created a new drinking occasion: the game pause. (Crucially, Core Design steered clear of having Lara

drink Lucozade in the game itself.) The TV spots were used in harness with an in-store campaign featuring life-size Laras, and on-pack promotions offering the chance to win *Tomb Raider* experiences. The closeness of the fit between celebrity and brand was underlined by a unique and bold move by Glaxo-SmithKline (Lucozade's parent company), which changed the name of the drink on the label to "Larazade" for a promotional period.

The partnership proved to be mutually reinforcing for all parties concerned: the association with Lara certainly boosted sales of Lucozade, which in turn helped to drive people to the *Tomb Raider* games. It also maintained Lara's presence in gamers' minds in the gap while the next game was being developed. Peter Harding, Brand Director at GlaxoSmithKline, was in no doubt about the effectiveness of the campaign, and told us at the time:

> "We've had double digit growth ever since we got involved with Lara – it's been a great success."

Janet Swallow, Senior VP of Lara Croft Merchandise at Eidos added:

> "It's given us terrific awareness and credibility and helped build Lara into a much stronger franchise."

However, there are still two mysteries about the Lara Croft story. The first is why the success of the Lucozade campaign has not been followed up with a flurry of Lara-endorsements in other categories.

Where is Lara's line of adventure wear? Why are there no other kinds of Lara game – like a driving game, for example? Where is the Lara-branded energy bar or fitness program or mountain bike? Again, perhaps she has been held back by her digital essence, even though she has signed-up with Los Angeles-based Creative Artists Agency (CAA) who have added the cyber-heroine to their list of celebrity clients. Over roughly the same period of time, Beckham's handlers have extracted maximum value from their property in a wide range of categories from sportswear to soft drinks to sunglasses. It seems very strange that Lara has never been leveraged in a similar way.

And the second Lara Croft mystery? Why is it that no other character since Lara has burst out of the screen to achieve the megastar status that will get consumers baying for its associated brands? It is impossible to believe that Lara's success was a one-off and yet several years down the road we are still waiting for a credible digital challenger for her crown – although a second big selling Eidos title, *Hitman*, (with charismatic main character Agent Codename 47) is to be made into a movie starring Vin Diesel.

Promotional tie-ups

Of course, marketeers have learnt lessons from Lara's success. There are now numerous examples of brands using promotional tie-ups linked to gaming, as well as borrowing from its look and iconography. For example, in early 2005 Fiat teamed up with Xbox to produce limited edition Stilo and Punto Xbox cars, which sported discreet Xbox logos throughout and shipped with a free console. They also offered consumers the opportunity to buy a pre-release version of the latest *Forza Motorsport* driving game. The promotion was presented in men's magazines using distinctive gaming artwork – vivid, luminescent backdrops, lava flows, fantasy creatures in flowing robes, futuristic streetscapes, and so on – to give the whole thing an authentic in-game feel. Similarly, Volvo launched their new S40 with TV ads that presented the car as if it were in a computer game, as a way of connecting with a target group that would respond positively to gaming's codes and conventions.

Product demos

Games also have the ability to demonstrate a product. When a Chrysler executive questioned the effectiveness of video games as a marketing medium, Jeff Bell of Jeep (who had no budget for TV or print) commissioned a bespoke online game, *Jeep 4x4: Trail of Life*. The game was free, and it was designed to give users a sense of the difference between a Rubicon Jeep (of which Chrysler expected to sell only 8000) and a standard Jeep, by replicating "the vehicle's axle ratios and horsepower torque." Within six months Jeff's decision had proved its worth, as some 250,000 consumers downloaded it and handed over their names and email addresses. The carmaker estimates that about 500 of the first 1500 people who purchased the Jeep Rubicon had piloted a virtual Jeep prior to visiting a dealership. Joel Schlader of Chrysler, characterizing the effectiveness of video games as advertising, declared:

**Jeep's virtual product trial for the Rubicon
was highly successful**

"It's shocking, [but] on the other hand, it's hardly surprising. It takes about 40 hours of playing to complete some popular adventure games and since ads are built into the games, consumers can't dodge them."

Sony Ericsson has also used this so-called "advergaming" to demonstrate the features of one of its mobile phones. The game requires players to use the in-game phone as a communication device and to capture an image using its built-in camera. Meanwhile, the US Army has given the idea a twist by building a virtual boot camp as a way of attracting new recruits.

There is huge potential for this kind of advergaming and we predict that this is only the start of things. According to Suhler Stevenson of research agency Veronis, the amount of time that Americans spend on gaming is doubling every five years and, in perhaps the surest sign of advergaming's looming legitimacy, video game publisher Activision is collaborating with market research company AC Nielsen "to build a system that will provide information about video games akin to TV ratings."

CRM

There is also a growing understanding of gaming's usefulness as part of a customer relationship management (CRM) strategy. For several years now the big media and fast-moving consumer goods (FMCG) brands have been using games as a way of attracting traffic to their websites and strengthening consumers' bond with the brand. These have often been very simple games aimed at pre-teens, while others have offered older audiences "quick fun and play" games, as well as competitions in exchange for information such as an email address and basic demographics. However, many of them are becoming more sophisticated and may involve ongoing updates and interaction as a way of encouraging a continuing relationship with the brand. Some even offer chatrooms to facilitate a dialogue between the users of the brand and, of course, an opportunity to gain insight into the needs of the consumer base. A quick look at a site such as the one Coca-Cola has developed for South Korea shows the kind of thing that can be done. This is perhaps the most sophisticated gaming audience in the world, and Coke has responded by producing a clutch of games clearly produced by top developers with a look, feel, and performance that builds respect and affinity for the brand.

Gaming event sponsorship

A few companies have already seen the commercial possibilities of gaming festivals such as the i-Series events that are held every couple of months at Newbury Racecourse in England. These events are attended by upwards of 2000 people who pack their towers, monitors, and keyboards, along with a tent, into the back of the car and head off for four days of non-stop gaming with fellow enthusiasts. The organizers provide the LAN arena, as well as campsites, showers, bars, and food stalls plus live entertainment provided by big name bands – while their commercial partners get a captive audience of young consumers for several days. So you may well find companies such as Microsoft, Ubisoft, and Codemasters giving festival-goers the opportunity of sampling their games in a non-competitive environment. As yet, though, non-gaming brands have not made an appearance at events such

An i-Series LAN festival in full swing

as these – which seems incredible when you think of the way that drinks and style brands compete for cool credentials and exposure at a music festival or a DJ event like Sonar. When are we to see gaming festivals regularly benefiting from the same level of sponsorship that their clubbing and rock counterparts enjoy? After all, the World Cyber Games has punched above its weight for its main sponsor Samsung for several years.

In-game advertising

Effective though all the techniques mentioned so far have been, they essentially used classic marketing techniques (celebrity endorsements, promo tie-ins, TV spots, event sponsorship, and the like), with gaming culture providing relevance and credibility. Today, however, most leading edge marketeers realize that one of the key challenges for brands in gaming is to go to a level beyond this and to gain exposure for brands by embedding them within the gameplay itself. This has proved easier said than done, as many gamers are highly cynical about the commercial world and are reluctant to countenance any sort of overt or intrusive branding. Perhaps this is a result of gaming's deep roots in creative and alternative communities, or the fact that so much of its cutting-edge tech and development work had been done by enthusiasts and academics, rather than by corporate-funded researchers. But there is no doubt that many gamers believe – even today – that gaming, both as an art form and as a shared experience, should be seen as a labor of love, not money, although that is inevitably slowly changing.

In this they show an attitude very similar to one commonly held in the literary world. Certainly, there were squeals of horror among literati in 2001, when the respected British novelist Fay Weldon published her new book *The Bulgari Connection*. The shock was not a response to the content or the quality of the writing, but to the fact that its author had accepted money from an Italian jeweler in return for the use of its name in the book's title and a number of favorable mentions of its products in the novel itself. For most literary folk the very thought of anything as vulgar as product placement in a novel was tantamount to apostasy, as Fay Weldon told *The New York Times*, when she spoke to them about the Bulgari deal:

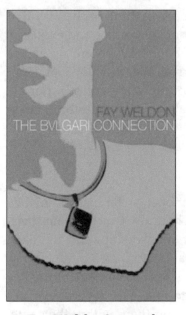

**Fay Weldon's novel
with paid-for
product placement**

"When the approach came through I thought, oh no, dear me, I am a literary author. You can't do this kind of thing; my name will be mud forever. But after a while I thought, I don't care. Let it be mud. They never give me the Booker prize anyway."

Although they might seem strange bedfellows, the comparison of gaming and literature is instructive in that it provides a few clues to ways in which brands might become acceptable within the gameplay. After all, readers are happy to accept it when writers name-check brands to give a heightened sense of reality to their work, but there seems to have been an unwritten law that to take money for doing so somehow tainted a novel's integrity and artistic merit. And, interestingly enough, the first appearances of brands in the gaming arena were more by accident than design, coming about simply as a by-product of developers' desire for realism. For example, gamers playing *FIFA* would expect to see the correct sponsors' names on their teams' shirts and "real" adverts on the boards around the grounds. It would somehow be weird to see Manchester United without "Vodafone" on their shirts – and plain naff to have made-up brand names on the hoardings around the stands. Equally, players of *Colin McRae Rally* would demand that their heroes drive the right brand of car, not an unbranded generic metal box. As a result of this, the brands themselves were mostly passive beneficiaries of free exposure – there was no stealth strategy on their part. But, of course, from here it was just a small step for brand owners to start managing their interests much more proactively.

Unsurprisingly, this is what has started to happen, although a concern for realism has still been a guiding principle in the more successful product placements. For a brand to intrude needlessly on

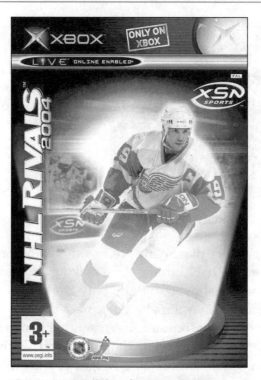

**Top sports titles feature sponsors'
names to add reality**

your virtual world and distract you from the fun in hand would be counterproductive in the extreme. But if, for example, you're going to jump into a taxi to go get a pizza, it sounds far more realistic to name your preferred pizza restaurant than to ask for a generic or leave it to the discretion of the driver, so in *Crazy Taxi* passengers will ask to be dropped off at Pizza Hut. In just the same way, if in the middle of a breathless armed chase through a hostile urban landscape, you choose to shelter from a hail of bullets behind a vending machine, it is only reasonable that it should be a branded one. And it makes perfect sense for games publishers to sell that media space to the highest bidder. Indeed, in online gaming, it is now possible to make these spaces "live," so that the ads change regularly, just as they would do on a billboard in the real world. Even the "No Logo" brigade among gaming purists seem to buy into the fact that this adds to the sense of authenticity, and accept that the revenue generated should also help to keep the prices of games down.

Why is this vending machine in the hugely popular *Half-Life* games not branded?

Certainly, product placement such as this is becoming increasingly common, with Electronic Arts making around $10 million from this kind of deal in 2004. But it only works for certain genres. Product placement in sports-based games will be largely determined by who the sponsors and advertisers happen to be in the real-life versions of the experience (although, of course, this significant extra exposure lends considerable weight to the original sponsorship deal), while in genres such as history and fantasy, product placement is far trickier – and in these areas, brands need to get a bit smarter. It would be incongruous for an action heroine to fight her way through a fantasy landscape, only to stop for a clearly branded drink. However, if she stopped for a non-branded energy-boosting drink which just happened to borrow its visual cues, codes, and iconography from a real world brand, that would be a different matter entirely and probably quite acceptable to most gamers.

Indeed, attempts at more overt brand exposure need to be handled with extreme caution. 7 Up is an example of a brand which has managed to do this effectively in the *SSX Tricky* snowboarding game, in which the player is surrounded by 7 Up billboards – although these are billboards with a difference. For much of the time the 7 Up logos are only partially visible or are distorted out of shape and they always occupy areas of the screen which would be at the periphery of the players' vision as they focus on the demanding business of playing the game itself. The result is akin to a subliminal prompt, which ensures that players don't feel they are being force-fed the brand.

The key point here is that corporate sponsors should never forget that mugging the punter with a logo-fest is simply not an option in this culture. In dealing with emerging youth-driven movements, many marketeers retain a false sense of hope from the ease with which the previous generation took a free ride on the back of rap. Who remembers that night back in March 1994 when Tommy Hilfiger famously persuaded up-and-coming rapper Snoop Doggy Dog to appear on prime-time *Saturday Night Live* dressed from cap to toe in clearly-labeled gear? (And all for just $15,000, so the story goes.) Sadly for marketeers, those days are long gone. The bragging culture of rap was the most brand-friendly manifestation of popular art forms since The Beach Boys boasted about their Honda or told us how much less fun life would be if Daddy took the T-Bird away. The gaming audience is quite a bit less amenable – or some would say, downright hostile.

This is certainly the case if McDonald's experience is anything to go by. They entered the gaming fray with the best of intentions and an utterly plausible strategy, and were one of the very first global brands to do so.

They identified the new online version of *The Sims*, published by Electronic Arts, as a suitable vehicle for their brand – which seemed like a shrewd move. In the game, players control characters in a virtual family as they interact with others in their local community. It appeals to all ages from pre-teens upwards, with more than half its players being female, and had already become the biggest selling PC game of all time with sales exceeding 19 million units. The idea was that when the subscription-based online version of the game launched in 2003, players would be given the chance to open their own McDonald's kiosk which would increase

**The Sims Online –
A pioneering tie-up with
McDonald's**

their skill, intelligence, and contentment ratings, as well as improving their game stats by consuming McDonald's products that they had purchased.

So far, so good. This seemed like a sensible way for McDonald's to connect to game players globally, to contemporize the brand, and to leverage its business reputation. However, they had made the mistake of assuming that gamers would be happy to play by their rules – and would perhaps even be grateful for their presence in the game. Certainly, they and Electronic Arts hadn't reckoned on the reaction of some elements of the gaming community. Even before it had been launched, a journalist for *PC Gamer* magazine wrote:

> *"The problem with the presence of McDonald's ... in The Sims Online lies in the heavy-handed manner of its implementation. Players are forced to jump through heavily branded hoops and penalized if they won't toe the corporate line. It is of little surprise, then, that we are witnessing a backlash from gamers against this intrusion into the gameplay even before the product has been launched."*

By integrating their kiosks into the fabric of *The Sims* life, McDonald's had shown that they had understood the immersive nature of the gaming experience, but they may have been less skilful in their judgment of the gaming culture, as many players saw McDonald's presence as an intrusion into their virtual world rather than an enhancement of the game. Gaming forums certainly documented a mixed response to McDonalds' arrival in the game, with some fans happy to see their game given greater mainstream credibility while others were less positive. One fan of *The Sims* wrote to the online *Gamespot Forum*, complaining:

> *"As long as it is ONLY window dressing (such as a billboard) that is fine. When it starts invading the gameplay, that's when I have a problem."*

Another website (Shift.com) went so far as to suggest that players should resort to guerrilla tactics against the brand to register their disapproval:

"Picket the nearest McDonald's kiosk. Stand in front of the kiosk and tell visitors why you think McDonald's sucks. ...

Actually order and consume virtual McD's food, then use The Sims Online's 'expressive gestures' in creative ways. Lie down and play dead. Emote the vomiting, sickness, or fatigue that might overcome you. ...

Open your own McDonald's kiosk. Verbally abuse all customers in the name of McDonald's. Loudly proclaim how terrible your food is and how it's made from substandard ingredients."

Worse still, a small number of disgruntled players started creating characters who were drug dealers, child prostitutes, and mobsters and making the local McDonald's their hang-out. And as quickly as their accounts were suspended or closed, others arrived to take their place.

Although by no means all the responses from the gaming community were hostile, McDonald's failure to understand gamers and gaming culture resulted in something of a PR backlash, despite their investing heavily in a brave and pioneering initiative. On the plus side, the phenomenal press coverage McDonald's received from their foray into the gaming world was probably sufficient in itself to render the exercise worthwhile from their point of view, if not 100 percent successful. Not all McDonald's experiences with gaming have been so unfortunate. They ran a successful campaign in 2003 offering exclusive online demos of *The Hobbit* game and giving away consoles in a gaming competition. They have also offered consumers simple Shockwave games which demonstrated a genuine understanding of gamers and their needs by making gaming cheaper and more accessible. Thus McDonald's have experienced the two extremes while dipping their corporate toe in the gaming water – no doubt learning valuable lessons along the way.

In-game commerce

On the other hand, when a brand can make itself useful and offer gamers a genuine service, there has been little resistance to its appearance within the gameplay. Domino's Pizza, for example, have devised a system whereby online gamers can walk into a virtual Domino's restaurant, order a pizza, pay by credit card, and get a real meal delivered to their real-life front door just a few minutes later – a boon for hungry gamers who don't want to leave the screen. In effect, Domino's are using online gaming as a new sales channel, an approach to in-game commerce which, if pursued sensitively, could generate all manner of opportunities for online traders in future – allowing them to sell anything from clothing to books to car accessories – as long as they remain relevant, helpful, and non-intrusive.

Conclusion: the seven ways of getting brands into gaming today

So far, then, in the brief history of brands in gaming, seven main marketing techniques have been developed:

- product endorsements by virtual celebrities such as Lara Croft
- promotional tie-ups using the codes and visual imagery of gaming to lend relevance and credibility to advertising in other media
- the use of games to demonstrate products and services
- gaming as a CRM tool, in particular its power to draw traffic to brand websites
- providing sponsorship or commercial partnership for gaming events and LAN parties
- in-game advertising, normally using media spaces that appear naturally in the course of the gameplay
- in-game commerce, in which the game is used as a new sales channel affording gamers opportunities to experience or even to buy relevant or useful products and services.

It should be stressed that these are still very early days and many new techniques will no doubt emerge. We will speculate about some of these later in the book, but next let's take a more detailed look at the gamers themselves and the communities to which they belong.

CHAPTER 4

All work and no play?

Culture and gaming

Hillary Clinton speaks her mind on video games

The demonization of gaming: debunking the myths

> *"Children are playing a game that encourages them to have sex with prostitutes and then murder them. This is a silent epidemic of media desensitization that teaches kids it's okay to diss people because they are a woman, they're a different color or they're from a different place."*

So said Democrat senator Hillary Clinton in a speech to a US childcare symposium in early 2005. She was talking about *Grand Theft Auto*, an 18-rated game in which players can peddle drugs, steal cars, and shoot people as they negotiate the mean streets of LA with the goal of becoming a top gangster. It might sound like the kind of material that most upstanding parents wouldn't want their darling teenage sons and daughters to be viewing on their computer screens. But does *Grand Theft Auto* really pose a threat to the "moral health" of its many millions of players, as the former First Lady would have us believe? Does stealing a car in a video game make you more likely to do so in real life? Does virtual violence really make people more aggressive away from the screen? ... Or could the complete opposite be the case? ... Or, indeed, might it have absolutely no effect on the player's "real life" behavior whatsoever?

If these concerns sound familiar, we need only look back to the mainstream uptake of video rentals, and indeed TV itself, to see exactly the same issues being raised. And as with these, you can dig up statistics to back up any side of the story. Researchers at the University of Oklahoma found that two-thirds of school fights were started by regular games players, but only 4 percent were started by children who had never played computer and video games. Then again, it might reasonably be supposed that there *are* only 4 percent of children who have never played computer and video games. Other studies showed that violent games would not cause serious problems in healthy families, but could do so in families where children were left alone for many hours. In 2005, a research team at the University of Aachen in Germany used magnetic resonance imaging (MRI) to scan the brains of young men playing video games and concluded that this kind of gaming triggers the same responses as actual aggression. It was suggested that as a result gamers would be more likely to respond aggressively when faced with violent situations in real life. But Dr Guy Cumberbatch of the UK's Communications Research Group took a very different view. When asked to comment, he said:

> "It's very much a witch-hunt in relation to video games. The instinct to punch someone on the nose is pretty basic. I don't think it is influenced in any way by playing these games."

As has been the case with sex and violence on TV and in the movies, this debate will no doubt run and run.

Right or wrong, though, Hillary Clinton's diatribe is symptomatic of a general unease in Western culture with the idea of gaming and play, at least among the rapidly dwindling number of non-gamers in the world. The media appears to delight in stereotypes that associate gamers with the darkest days of (usually male) adolescence, presenting them as foul-smelling, wordless, lazy, friendless sociopaths. Adult gamers are, by extension, stigmatized as sad, emotionally stunted arrested developers. We are constantly told that gaming promotes violence, or that it causes obesity or reduces children's IQs, or that it endorses anti-social behavior and encourages idleness and time-wasting. The most recent edition of the American parenting bible, *Dr Spock's Baby and Childcare*, has this to say about computer and video games:

> "The best that can be said of them is that they may help to promote eye–hand co-ordination in children. The worst that can be said is that they sanction and even promote aggression and violent responses in conflict. But what can be said with much greater certainty is this: most computer games are a colossal waste of time."

What on earth could have provoked such a gale of derision? After all, gamers are not known for mugging grannies in alleys to finance their habit, or keeping the neighbors awake until three am or throwing up noisily in public spaces. In fact, there is a growing body of theory and research which points to the fact that gaming improves a wide range of high-order cognitive skills, such as problem solving and systems analysis, as well as prediction based on probability theory, pattern recognition, and spatial geometry. That might sound high falutin', but there is something going on here, as you can see if you look at the figures for American IQ tests. Between 1943 and 2001, average American IQ scores rose by 17 points at a rate of 0.31 points per year. However, what is instructive is that this increase was not at a steady rate, but part of a curve that climbed steeply in the 1990s to 0.36 points per year – exactly the same period in which computer and video games were gaining a hold on the nation's leisure habits. The IQ score gain was most marked in tests for abstract reasoning and pattern recognition, two skills which we might expect practiced gamers to perform well at. Of course, this doesn't prove that gaming leads to an improved IQ – there are many other factors which might account for it – but there are grounds for suspecting that there might be a link. This suspicion is supported by a study of 700 children conducted in 2002 by researchers funded by the UK government's Department for Education and Skills who found that computer games improved problem-solving skills, concentration, memorization, and collaboration.

CEO TEASER
**Which emergent consumer group boasts a
majority who take regular and vigorous exercise?**

A recent survey sponsored by the Entertainment Software Association (ESA) also dispels the myth that gamers are sedentary and overweight. The survey conducted by Peter D. Hart Research Associates, randomly polled 802 adults and found that among those who spent 6.8 hours or more per week playing games, 70 percent exercise or play sport for an average of 20 hours or more per month. Douglas Lowenstein, President of the ESA, concluded that:

> *"Those who continue to portray the game population as loafers are living in their own fantasy world."*

So why have the positive aspects of gaming been so wilfully disregarded? Why should having a blast on an Xbox or chilling out with *The Sims* provoke such extreme scorn?

The answer probably lies at the heart of the work ethic which has shaped industrial and post-industrial societies for nigh-on two centuries. For generations, the distinction between "work" and "leisure" has lain at the core of the Western value system. For Protestant-influenced societies like the USA, the UK, Scandinavia, and northern Germany, in particular, work and virtue were explicitly linked. Hard work led directly to serious reward – terrestrial, heavenly, or preferably both. A roll of banknotes in the back pocket wouldn't necessarily guarantee admission through St Peter's Gates, but it sure as hell suggested that somebody up there liked you.

The flipside of this was the marginalization of leisure. Let's face it, if you were re-engineering human life on a blank sheet of paper, you'd give leisure a pretty high rating wouldn't you? How many days would you like ideally? Five out of seven? Six? The lot? But somehow the Protestants got themselves into the kind of work–life crisis in which leisure was squeezed out of the picture altogether and life ended up as nothing but work, work, work. Leisure, when it finally emerged, was something to be compartmentalized into weekends or evenings, or enjoyed on the golf course by deserving retirees in the few years before they met their virtuous end. In short, paid work was the business of life and not to work was to deny the purpose of existence. This spawned a culture in which the unpaid labor of millions of housewives could be trivialized and dismissed, in which children were better seen than heard, and in which the unemployed were considered scarcely human. In this world, sport might have been an acceptable pastime for "real" working men ... and perhaps the odd woman, too ... but games? Oh, come on ... they were definitely for kids.

Over the past 20 years or so, though, things have started to change. On the one hand, work has invaded the leisure space to an unprecedented degree. The financial-services-Mom who sleeps with her Blackberry under the pillow and packs the kids off to capoeira camp at weekends so she can take a few extra meetings is only too real. But, on the other hand, leisure has started to seep back into work. Suddenly, enthusiasms have morphed into careers. After all, how many people now do regular work simply to get seed money to set themselves up as designers, DJs, jewelers, or chiropractors? How many of us know someone who has chafed against a dismal job for years while nursing an eccentric hobby, only to transform that hobby into a lucrative source of income by finding thousands of fellow enthusiasts worldwide on the Internet?

Could it now be the case that many post-industrial societies have reached a tipping point in their understanding of the relationship between work and leisure? As work moves from coal face to mind space, from production line to online, from knowing the right names to playing the right games, could it be that the paradigm has shifted too?

Cultural mega-trends in the rise of gaming

If it is indeed the case that the paradigm has shifted, then gaming can be seen as emblematic of the way in which societies are changing – and may even prove to be instrumental in the process as well. Let's take a look at four social mega-trends that gaming captures and expresses in a way no other cultural phenomenon appears to do: intensity, affinity, nostalgia, and the commoditization of technology.

There is no doubt that across the developed world there is a yearning for intensity and an impatience with the everyday and the mundane. For young men, in particular, this is sometimes characterized as an atavistic ache for the thrill of battle which, to most, is now only available vicariously through pale metaphors and substitutes. But the feeling is definitely not restricted to young men alone. For decades, TV and movies, music and sport have bathed everyone in myths and imagery of intense experiences of triumph, failure, sex, violence, death, love, companionship, and so on. And yet for many in the developed world, the reality of life has been: home – car – office – car – home – TV – bed. Against this backdrop, the appeal of a multi-sensory gaming experience which casts the player as an all-action hero is only too obvious. Indeed, with Hollywood movies taking less and less at the box office as the multiplex is pushed aside by home entertainment systems, for many people the choice of entertainment for an evening in is starting to come down to a stark choice between a movie on DVD or a gaming session. And sophisticated narrative-driven games like *Half-Life 2* are well-placed to win this argument, as they offer a movie-like experience (but with many more hours' viewing for the money), plus the key attraction of the chance for the viewer to step into the starring role him- or herself to dictate the action and affect the outcome.

We are also seeing the emergence of so-called affinity communities – lifestyle clusters based on common interests such as cars, fashion, or sport – in which individuals can shrug off the identity imposed on them in their working or domestic life. In the past, people might have tried to express the urge to do this by belonging to a society or a club – the Harley-Davidson Owners, perhaps, or a local wargaming association. But this would probably have entailed regular meetings and yet another narrowly defining social circle. Today, however, people can flit between several different identities in different gaming communities in a single evening, meeting people from all over the world online. Equally, they can adopt a number of different roles in various ongoing games. In this sense, gaming can offer a true liberation from the straitjacket in which so many people find themselves trapped.

There is also an urge to romanticize the past, a nostalgia for a more comfortable age that celebrated individual style and originality. In part, this is a response to the perception that we live in

**Gordon Freeman, star of the
BAFTA award-winning
game *Half-Life 2*
(with accomplice Alyx Vance)**

dangerous times; as fear of street crime, burglary, random attack, and terrorism increases, we look back more fondly on what are perceived as the security and certainties of bygone ages. But this nostalgia is also a backlash against a society that deals increasingly in categories and genres, making people feel they are too easily pigeonholed by their occupation, clothes, tastes, or lifestyle choices. The result is a strong desire to participate in arenas in which individuals are free to define themselves and not be pinned down by other people's preconceptions. Gaming offers a perfect way of meeting these needs, enabling people to explore other times and spaces from the safety of the living room, to shake off personal baggage, to adopt roles, and to make choices about how they appear to others. Gaming also fulfils the desire to recreate the best moments of our youth – and increasingly these are embedded in gaming experiences.

Finally, the absorption of new technologies into the mainstream of everyday life has raised everyone's expectations of what they can expect from entertainment media and has rendered traditional leisure pursuits disappointingly one-dimensional. TV now seems too passive and unresponsive, movies too pompous and remote, radio and music have become background-only, while traditional nightlife experiences like pubbing and clubbing seem parochial in comparison with the wide world opened up by the Internet. Small wonder, then, that more and more people are turning to gaming for thrills, challenge, and a new sense of themselves as part of a genuinely switched-on global community.

Pathways to friendship

The central role of gaming in the creation and development of new communities is one of the most interesting and potentially far-reaching of its many benefits. Despite the best efforts of gaming's detractors to portray it as a lonely activity, it is clear that for many gamers – perhaps for the majority – gaming is anything but a solitary pursuit. For some, it might mean hanging out and playing games at the local Internet café or LAN arena. For others, it might mean getting a group of friends together at someone's house or flat to spend a few hours huddled around a console or PC attempting to best one another on a favorite sports game or shoot 'em up or better one another's scores on a dance mat. In these cases, gaming will keep a group of friends together by providing the occasion, the context, and the lubricant for a social event.

More intriguing, though, is the way that online games are creating new opportunities to meet people and develop new friendships and communities. At the most basic level, these are virtual friendships, forged while playing a team game online and developed by exchanging feedback, tips, and personal information in a chatroom after the game has finished. Many players will have 30 or 40 such virtual friends with whom they play and chat regularly online, and who may come from different countries all round the world. But we are increasingly seeing how these virtual friendships develop into real friendships pursued over a drink and a handshake as well as a keyboard and a mouse ...

Meet Craig, who's a car mechanic from Melbourne in Australia, and another guy called Yoshi. They are both part of a group that has been meeting regularly online over the past few weeks to play *World of Warcraft*. They've exchanged comments and quips in the chatroom a few times, but Craig had always assumed that Yoshi was based in Japan, because of his name. Then he notices something interesting about Yoshi's ping time. In technical terms, the ping shows the packet data upload speed, but in practical terms, it can help to identify roughly how close another player is to you (provided you are armed with certain information like the other player's Internet connection speed). The more similar the ping, the closer you are likely to be to one another geographically. When Craig takes this up with Yoshi, it emerges that Yoshi is an Aussie too – he turns out to be an accountant based in Sydney and is planning on visiting Melbourne later that month. Craig and Yoshi get together over a beer and real friendship is born, one that they can sustain through a common interest in gaming and regular meetings at gaming competitions across Australia.

Thousands of friendships have already been made this way, friendships that cut across professional and social divides and obliterate geographical and cultural differences. These are the kind of friendships that could only have been forged in the past by backpackers who spent their gap years Inter-railing or those who went on exchanges or summer camps; in short, the fortunate few. Today, thanks to the new social channels and comradely glue that gaming offers, friendships like these are available to all.

Conclusion: play's revenge

Most of us are now numb to the clichés about how life is becoming faster, busier, more stressful, and ever more demanding. And it is generally accepted that much of the blame for this can be attributed to new technologies. The helter-skelter development in computing, the Internet, and mobile telephony in recent years has all been driven by the need to work more efficiently and quickly than ever before. How ironic, then, that the very same technologies are now being used to empower the countervailing force – the re-emerging need to play. The very machines that in the 1990s threatened to turn us all into isolated, desk-bound, workaholic box tickers have now been repurposed to allow us to connect with each other through gaming and to slip away from those pressures, to learn more about ourselves through play, to create and collaborate, to challenge and compete, to relax and refresh ourselves in other worlds. No wonder that so many people are switching on to the immersive, benignly addictive lure of gaming. But who exactly are they? It's time to find out.

CHAPTER 5

Behind the avatar

Who plays games?

Who is gaming and how much?

Once you get past the gamer stereotypes, it quickly becomes apparent that the category "gamers" is huge and extremely diverse. In particular, the idea that gamers are all teenage boys or younger 20-somethings is clearly wrong. Our research, based on interviews with over a thousand people in the UK and Germany, showed that gaming is popular with both sexes of all ages, from toddlers to their grandparents! It is true that gamers of school and college age enjoy more gaming sessions per week on average – over six sessions per week in the UK, as Figure 5.1 (Who is gaming today and how much?) shows – but this result would be expected, as these are the two groups with the most leisure time. What is particularly interesting is that older people are not so far behind in terms of the average number of gaming sessions, with consumers in the 35+ age groups still having about four sessions per week.

It might also be expected that gaming sessions would tend to become shorter, as people become older – and so, presumably, busier. Our research shows that this is indeed the case, as can be seen in Figure 5.2 (For how long do people game?), with the average length of a session lasting around an hour and a half for younger gamers and falling to just over an hour for people in middle age. But, again, it should be noted that these are significant amounts of leisure time for all ages concerned, and so present marketeers with a golden opportunity to reach out not just to younger consumers but to people of all ages.

Figure 5.1

Source: Added Value/B.I.G. proprietary research

Women in gaming

There has also long been the perception that gaming is a male-dominated pursuit. Up to a point this is still correct, with women in the UK, for example, accounting for only 27.2 percent of all active gamers. However, this male bias has nothing to do with the intrinsic nature of gaming itself, but is rather a legacy of the way in which the industry has developed. Historically, female take-up of computer science and related engineering courses has been low;

Figure 5.2

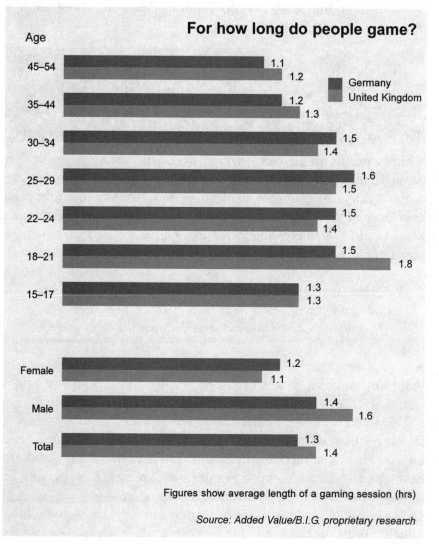

For how long do people game?

Figures show average length of a gaming session (hrs)

Source: Added Value/B.I.G. proprietary research

even today women account for only 20 percent of UK computer science undergraduates, with similarly low figures in most other developed countries. With so few women with the necessary skills and training to enter the business, it is inevitable that games developers have been predominantly male; in fact, women make up only 17 percent of the games industry's workforce in the UK today. The result of this has been that male games developers have tended to design games that reflect their own interests and enthusiasms – hence the preponderance of action, sports games, and shoot 'em ups in many games publishers' catalogs.

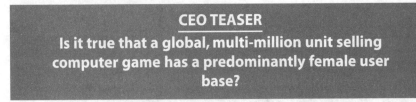

CEO TEASER
Is it true that a global, multi-million unit selling computer game has a predominantly female user base?

However, as more women become involved in games design (something which government initiatives in several countries are encouraging), so games will become more female-friendly. The development team of *The Sims Online*, for example, was 40 percent women and it is interesting to see that 60 percent of its players are now female. Jessica Lewis, the game's producer has said:

> *"I think simply because more women are involved in the design and development, a different kind of contribution happens. Diversity ... is a good thing when making a mainstream game."*

So, as more women become involved in the industry, it is inevitable that more games appealing to women will be produced, creating a virtuous circle which will suck still more women into gaming.

This trend will be reinforced by some of the other developments in gaming that we have already noticed. Women already outnumber men as players of mobile games and simple online games, and are now starting to make up a significant percentage of players in MMORPGs (massively multi-player online role-playing games) such as *EverQuest*. As mobile and online gaming grow – something which looks certain to happen over the next few years – the involvement of women in gaming will increase sharply. Indeed, mobile phone games company I-play estimates that, currently, 80 percent of its 5 million players in Europe are female.

The needs that gaming meets

The role that gaming plays in the lives of both men and women varies enormously. For some, gaming is a social bonding experience that brings friends together to compete with each other and have fun. Others will see gaming as a way of expressing themselves, trying out new things, and responding to personal challenges. Figure 5.3 (Mapping the gaming needs) plots the main needs that gaming addresses. The axis of inner-directed to outer-directed indicates the degree to which it fulfils people's social needs, while the axis of wind-up to wind-down shows the extent to which it offers relaxation or excitement. Compare this to Figure 5.4 (Which types of game genre deliver against which needs?), and you have a first cut of the way in which particular game genres can be used to reach particular groups or individuals on particular occasions. So, for example, a sports game like *FIFA* would appeal to groups of friends who want to meet up and enjoy themselves in the spirit of friendly competition. An online first-person shooter like *Counter-Strike* would fulfill a similar social need but would be taken far more seriously by people looking for thrills and intense competition. On the other hand, people who want to relax by themselves in front of the screen after work might choose a simulation game like *The Sims* or *RollerCoaster Tycoon*.

The main types of gamer

So, as we have already seen, the term "gamer" encompasses many different types of people: hardcore enthusiasts who have turned gaming into their profession, young professionals unwinding after a long day at the office, kids vying to out-cool each other in the play-ground, bored young mums playing *Snake* on their mobile phones while waiting for the bus ... the list goes on. So next, let's try to break this huge category down into its main typologies, which can be seen in Figure 5.5 (Who plays games?). The figure shows the importance of gaming in people's lives on the axis of life central to peripheral, and the extent to which it fulfils people's social needs on the axis of inner-directed to outer-directed.

The eight main gaming types we have identified are as follows:

- Clansmen
- Masters of the universe
- Boys into gaming
- Older boys into gaming

Figure 5.3

Mapping the gaming needs

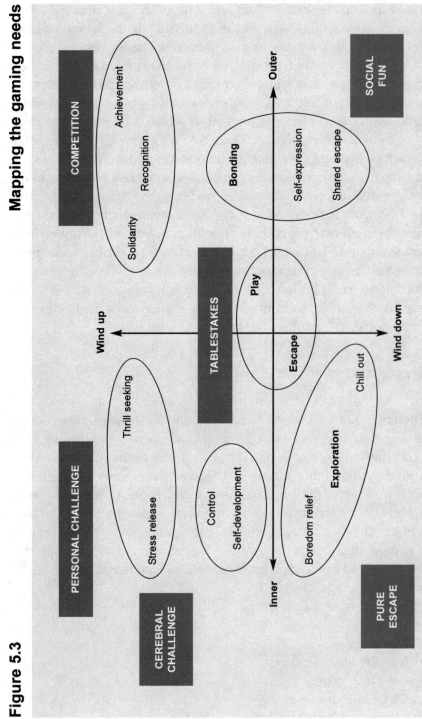

Figure 5.4   Which types of game genre deliver against which needs?

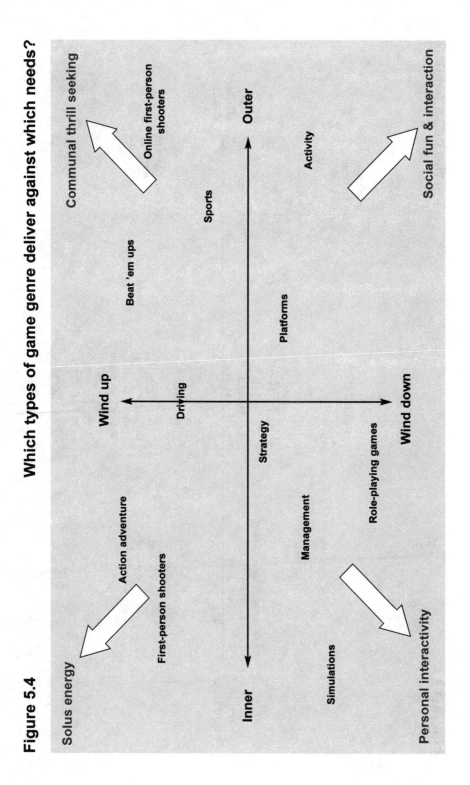

Solus energy

Communal thrill seeking

Online first-person shooters

Action adventure

First-person shooters

Beat 'em ups

Sports

Activity

Wind up

Outer

Driving

Strategy

Platforms

Inner

Wind down

Management

Role-playing games

Simulations

Personal interactivity

Social fun & interaction

Figure 5.5

Who plays games?

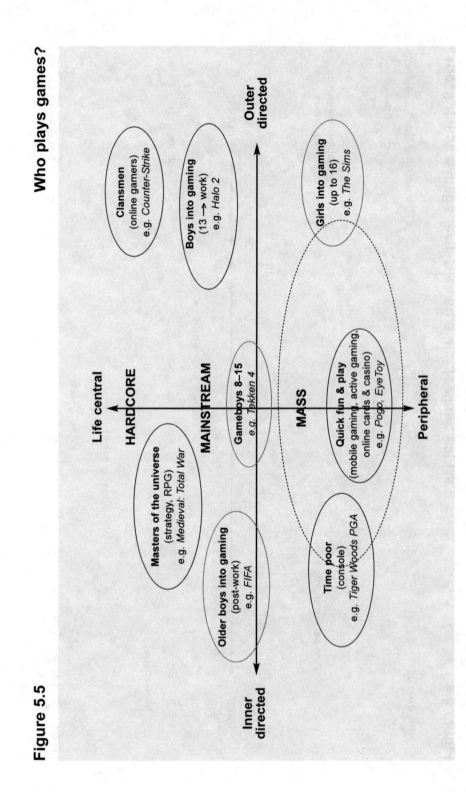

- Gameboys
- Girls into gaming
- Time poor
- Quick fun and play.

Let's now take a closer look at these groups of people and their relationships with gaming.

Clansmen

"I want gaming to be taken seriously as a real sport. See, I know I'm good, but now I want to test myself against the best."

We call the really hard-core gamers, Clansmen. These need not necessarily be professionals like the 4 Kings and the Lemmings that we met in Chapter 2, but they are still extremely committed and highly skilled gamers who play for at least an hour every weekday, followed by marathon sessions (sometimes lasting as long as 12 hours and more at a stretch) in the company of friends at weekends. Typically, these are guys in the 15–35 age range, with a job which is often IT-related. Although they may do quite a bit of their gaming at home, their focus is very much on gaming as a competitive sport and social activity. Broadly speaking, they divide into two categories: those who are members of clans and favor online first-person shooters such as *Unreal Tournament* and *Counter-Strike,* and those who belong to guilds whose preference is for MMORPGs like *EverQuest* and *World of Warcraft.* As well as their close buddies in their own clan or guild, they will know many other online regulars. They may meet some of these people at gaming tournaments, while others they may never see face to face, although they will often hook up with them in a chatroom after a game.

Masters of the universe

"I pride myself on being one step ahead and in the know."

Our next type of gamer, the Master of the universe, belongs to an altogether more elusive breed. Probably in the 25–40 age group, in full time work and living alone or in accommodation shared with friends, these are people who tend to play solo on PCs (or increasingly on consoles as a new generation of these platforms offers much improved processing power) and they use gaming as a means of stress relief and escape. They like games that offer challenges and opportunities for exercising control and mastery, so they often choose fantasy, historical, or narrative-driven games with an intellectual edge, such *Medieval: Total War*, *Star Wars: Empire At War*, or *Civilization 4*. These may be turn-based games or, more usually, real-time strategy games. In the past these were normally for solo play, but online multi-player versions of these games are now catching on. Another popular category for Masters of the universe is sports strategy, soccer being far and away the most popular, with *Championship Manager 4/5* and *Football Manager 2006* among the top titles. However, they can also opt to manage anything from a Tour de France cycling team to a stable of thoroughbred racehorses. And the Masters of the universe are certainly no less passionate about their gaming than their brothers and sisters in the clans and guilds. Many of them will come home from work and play for two to four hours every evening, with longer sessions at weekends, often comparing their progress to that of their friends or other online strategists and managers.

Boys into gaming

"I love playing games with my mates: the best nights are when they all come round and we have a good session together."

Moving right into the middle of the mainstream, we find Boys into gaming, guys in the 13–21 age group, for whom gaming is a key part of their social lives and group bonding rituals. For them, the best gaming experiences are to be found in those titles which bring people together and give them the chance to battle it out with each other. Take a typical young British guy called Joe. He's 18, lives with his parents and is studying at college for his "A" levels. His idea of a great night out is to meet up with his mates at one of their houses (usually the one with the best hardware) to play a few matches of the latest football simulation, such as *FIFA* or *Pro Evolution Soccer*. They may then head off for a few drinks followed by a club before going back to somebody's house for a gaming session on PlayStation or Xbox that will last until dawn. He'll play a fairly wide variety of games in these chill-out sessions, from beat 'em ups like *Def Jam Vendetta* to driving adventures like *Getaway*, from sports simulations like *Tony Hawk's Underground* to first-person shooters like *Halo: Combat Evolved*. When he is on his own, he will sometimes play these games against the computer in order to hone his skills, but his main motivation for doing this will be to increase his chances of beating his mates next time they meet up.

Older boys into gaming

"The closer a game is to reality, the more intense it is."

The next group are the ones who haven't got the stamina to see in the dawn like they used to: Older boys into gaming. Between 21 and 28 years of age, these are guys in full time work who are living alone or with friends or who may still be living with their parents, having not yet flown the nest or having returned home after university. They'll use gaming to unwind by themselves at home after work and will occasionally get together with the boys to play a few mainstream games, just like they used to in the good old days. Once in a while they'll get really involved in a new game and go on a solo marathon session. Many of these gamers are in a transitional phase between gaming with friends on social occasions and using gaming as a way of finding new friends and communities online. In other words, they are yesterday's mainstream social gamer and tomorrow's mainstream online solo/virtual social gamer. Some have the potential to become hardcore gamers, while others may drift towards the Quick fun and play typology.

Gameboys

"Me and my mates are always arguing about who's the coolest gaming character, who's the fastest finger, that kind of stuff."

Also close to the middle of the mainstream are the Gameboys: 8 to 13-year-olds who'll hang out in the corner of the playground with their mates boasting about their top scores, swapping "cheats," lending each other the hottest new games and telling stories about last night's gaming adventures. Portable platforms like Nintendo's Game Boy are popular, as gaming sessions are normally unplanned and just fit in with whatever else they happen to be doing, like chilling out after school or riding in the passenger seat of their mum's car. There's no doubt that there's a keen interest in games that flirt with sex and embrace violence, but the most popular games in this category are the fast action platformers such as *Sonic* and *Mario*. There's also considerable kudos attached to owning the latest hardware (Nintendo's DS and Game Boy Micro as well as Sony's PSP are the current "must haves"), as well as peripherals like slip cases (tailored pouches fitted with a belt loop to carry your gaming device), game cartridge cases (another kind of pouch for transporting a game, which might fit onto a key ring), or in-car adaptors, which plug into a car's cigarette lighter to keep the device charged when on the move.

Girls into gaming

> "Girls just wanna have fun – that's why more and more of us are getting into gaming."

On the other side of the playground are the Gameboys' female counterparts: the Girls into gaming. For them, gaming is sociable and competitive. They'll get together with friends around a PlayStation 2 to play creative strategy games like *The Sims* or action adventures like *The Legend of Zelda*. Or they'll get out the dance mat, load up *DDRMAX: Dance Dance Revolution* and vie with each other for the highest score and the coolest moves. Once in a while, they'll take on the boys at a more male-oriented game like *Gran Turismo* just to demonstrate a bit of girl-power.

Time poor

> "I love playing games but I don't really get the time to play any more."

And what about the Dads? Typically, these are the Time poor. Let's take the example of David (44), who's an accountant. He owns a laptop and has bought his children an Xbox 360. He only plays games occasionally and doesn't take them too seriously, even though he has to admit he is hoping to finish *Halo: Combat Evolved*, as he has developed a taste for it after playing it as a means of spending more time with his kids. His gaming sessions are likely to be fairly short – less than an hour – but on the odd occasion when his wife is out with friends and he's got the kids to bed at a reasonable hour, he'll have a longer spell in the virtual cockpit of an airplane in his favorite flight simulator. He also enjoys playing a round of golf on one of the world's most exclusive (and expensive) courses through the latest in the *Links* series of golf simulators and he's thinking of investing in a Gametrak controller and a copy of *Real World Golf* so that he can hook up his golf clubs to his computer and improve his swing – far cheaper and more convenient than having to go to the course itself!

Quick fun and play

"I get really bored when I'm hanging around or traveling; playing games gives me something to do."

David's wife is more likely to fit into the same gaming category as her parents: the Quick fun and play. These are people in the 35–65 age bracket, who are seeking a break from routine, a quick thrill, or a way of killing a few dull moments. This might mean no more than a game of Solitaire on the office computer during a coffee break, but it could mean an online game of bridge or even a flutter on a hand of poker at an online casino. They might also be tempted by a mobile phone game to distract them on the commute or while waiting for the plane to take them off on holiday. One of the most popular games with this group is the simple but addictive *Hearts*, a card game which ships with just about every new PC. Crucially, this has the three key characteristics which this group looks for in a game: it is immediately accessible through easily navigable menus, it has simple game mechanics and rules so that it's easy to play, and it can be played for as long or as short a time as you wish, so that it can be made to fit in with any kind of lifestyle.

Of course, as Figure 5.6 shows, there is a considerable amount of movement from one type to another. A Gameboy may grow up into a Clansman; a Master of the universe may get married and suddenly become Time poor; a Girl into gaming may leave school, get a job, and drift into the Quick fun and play group. But the key thing to note is that there is no marked drop-off in the number of gamers as they age – they simply drift from one type to another. The message for brands is a happy one. An investment in gaming is not simply a way of targeting youth; it is an opportunity for a brand to grow with its consumers and remain relevant over a whole lifetime.

Gaming occasions

So what about the occasions on which all these different types of people game? Figure 5.7 (Gaming occasions) gives our take on the most significant ones for all the types described above. Some of these occasions sit comfortably with our traditional expectations of media consumption, and indeed, in many households gaming may occur in parallel with TV viewing at certain times of day. So, for both Gameboys and Girls into gaming, one of the main gaming occasions will be the after-school period, when they might well game with children's TV running in the background. Older boys into gaming may well favor gaming in the evening to change gear after a hard day's work. But many gaming occasions are missed by the normal media radar altogether. The early hours/twilight zone represents a major social gaming occasion for groups such as Boys into gaming and Clansmen, but is a time of day that is normally dismissed as the "insomniac hours" by traditional media. Equally, mobile gaming throws up all kinds of unpredictable occasions – waiting in reception areas, queuing for tickets, sitting on buses – which have yet to be adequately identified and targeted.

Conclusion: couch potato no more

So, the reality of today's gamers is far removed from the gamer stereo-types, the friendless nerd and the overweight couch potato. Over the

Figure 5.6

Typology evolution

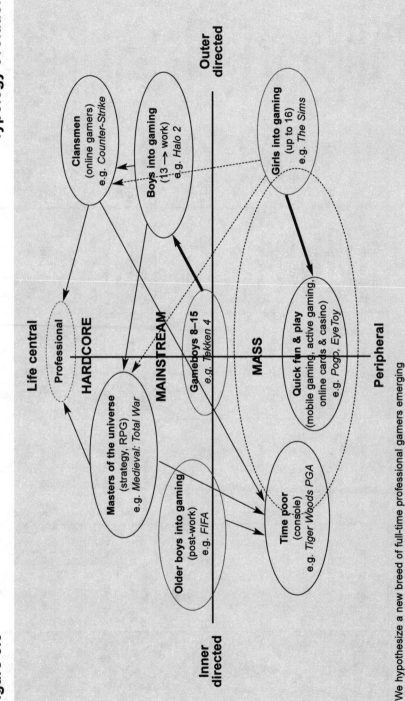

We hypothesize a new breed of full-time professional gamers emerging

Figure 5.7

Gaming occasions

Key gaming occasions	After school	After work	In a break	Social blast (post study/work, pre-going out)	On the go (mobile)	Marathon all-nighter (planned or spontaneous)
Who (consumer typologies)	Boys into gaming Girls into gaming Gameboys Solus/small groups	Older boys into gaming Masters of the universe Clansmen Solus occasion	Boys into gaming Girls into gaming Gameboys Quick fun & play Solus occasion	Boys into gaming Older boys into gaming Girls into gaming Clansmen (virtual) Group occasion (2–5)	All groups but especially Gameboys (handhelds) Quick fun & play Girls into gaming Boys & Older boys into gaming (mobile) Solus/pairs	Boys into gaming Older boys into gaming Clansmen Masters of the universe (solus) Group occasion (3–8)
Where	In home or friend's home	In home	In home, at work	In home or friend's home	While travelling or waiting for friends	In home or friend's home
Why (key needs)	Escape/play Bonding Recognition (m) Self-expression (f)	Stress relief Self development Control Achievement Solidarity	Escape Boredom relief Exploration Chill out	Bonding Thrill seeking Solidarity Recognition Shared escape	Boredom relief Escape Stress relief Time kill	Bonding Thrill seeking Solidarity Stress release
Length of occasion	0.5–1.5 hours	1.5–2 hours	10–60 mins	1–3 hours	5 mins–2 hours	2–8 hrs +
Frequency of occasion	5 days a week	2–3 nights a week	Up to 3–4 times per day	Once a week (Boys) Once a fortnight (Older boys)	Varies from 2–3 times a day to once a week	Once a week (Boys into gaming) Occasional (Older boys into gaming)

next few years, there is no doubt that gaming will become even more socially acceptable – both as a topic of everyday conversation and as a fun way to spend time with friends. It will certainly be viewed as a far more dynamic and engaging leisure activity than watching TV or listening to the radio. The spread of dedicated gaming cafes and LAN arenas will underline its social credentials and, with broadband-enabled computers becoming an increasingly indispensable part of everyday life, it seems certain that gaming will move even further into the cultural mainstream. This process will be accelerated by the convergence of film, music, TV, and gaming properties which will offer consumers more choice, greater flexibility, and higher quality at lower prices than today. The future for gaming and gamers looks bright indeed, as we'll find out in the next chapter.

CHAPTER 6

Hankook Igyora!

The future of gaming

Gaming in South Korea

"Hankook Igyora!" (roughly translated as "Win, Korea!") was the chant of the ecstatic fans in the stadia, city squares, and shopping malls of Seoul, Pusan, and Kwangju as they watched the South Korean football team defy all expectations to reach the semi-finals of the 2002 World Cup. To judge from such wild enthusiasm, you might have guessed that soccer was *the* South Korean national game. But you would have been wrong. And in case you're guessing, no, it isn't tae kwon do or ssireum either. There's absolutely no doubt about it, the national sport of South Korea is gaming.

The South Korean peninsula is the cutting edge of the gaming world, with computer and video gaming at the heart and soul of the social scene. There are four television channels devoted exclusively to gaming, broadcasting 24/7, and the results of the latest gaming competitions are reported on the main channels straight after the news, just as football or basketball might be elsewhere. A professional gamer, like Hong Jin-Ho – or "Thunder Zerg" as he's known in cyberspace – is a true mega-star (think David Beckham or Kris Benson) with a six-figure annual income and a 200,000-member fan club. In fact, gaming is the single most popular pastime among South Korean adults, who regularly eschew bars and nightclubs in favor of the many giant LAN arenas throughout the country, in which more than a thousand PCs will be networked.

In this chapter, we're going to look at five key areas in the future development of gaming:

1. Online gaming.
2. Mobile gaming.
3. Active gaming.
4. Professional gaming.
5. Augmented-reality gaming.

So to find out what's happening in the first of these, let's hop on a flight to the South Korean capital of Seoul.

Online gaming

Part of the reason for the popularity of gaming in South Korea is that the country is on a different planet when it comes to broadband access. The basic 512Kbps connection and pay-as-you-go dial-up services are not even available there any more. Their entry level broadband connection speed is a staggering 20Mbps, with most residential subscribers opting for the standard 50Mbps service. Compare this with the connection speed of 1 or 2 Mbps, which is currently the fastest available to home users in the UK, or the top speed of 5Mbps available to North American subscribers. And in South Korea, access to broadband Internet services is pretty much mandatory, with 13.5 million high-speed hubs in a country with a population of 48 million – representing a 72 percent household penetration (compared with 35 percent in Japan, and just 21 percent in the UK).

All this bandwidth has led to South Korea's wildly enthusiastic uptake of PC-based online games, in particular, those known as MMORPGs. These differ from online games such as *Return To Castle Wolfenstein* not only in genre, but also in the sense that they are truly "massive." An online game such as *Wolfenstein* might typically accommodate perhaps 32 players and last somewhere between three and eight minutes with gaming sessions continuing for an hour to an hour and a half. An MMORPG, on the other hand, offers gamers the chance to control a character – or avatar – in a perpetual online world, simultaneously inhabited by thousands and thousands of other characters all controlled by other gamers. The current leader of the MMORPG pack in Europe and the US is a game called *World of Warcraft*, which is run by publisher Blizzard Entertainment. In less than a year it boasted in excess of 4 million regular paying subscribers

World of Warcraft
(World of Warcraft® and Blizzard Entertainment®,
provided courtesy of Blizzard Entertainment, Inc.)

worldwide, with over 800,000 in Europe alone, within the first six months of its European launch, while South Korea's most popular MMORPG, NCsoft's all-conquering fantasy game *Lineage*, has a user base in excess of 2.5 million players just in South Korea! In *Lineage*, gamers control princes, wizards, and elves who fight to the death in mini-armies – or guilds – as they try to gain control of castles that dot its virtual world. The winners can then earn virtual money by levying feudal taxes on the villages under their control or charging other characters a percentage on weapons sales. What is remarkable is that this virtual commercial world has generated a parallel market in the real world, with virtual items such as magical swords changing hands on Korean websites for hard real-world cash. In fact, so lucrative has this trade become that there are even rumors that organized crime syndicates are moving in on the scene.

The appeal of MMORPGs is obvious. They have the same compelling nature as a TV soap opera, with a huge cast of characters – some familiar, others new – living through dramatic events in an ongoing persistent world. The crucial difference with an MMORPG is that you are utterly immersed because you are in control of one of the characters. Most people find it very hard to resist having a quick peek to see what is happening to their online avatar several times a day. In fact, there have been scare stories about some people finding this kind of game dangerously addictive. In one extreme case back in October 2002, 24-year-old Kim Kyung-jae collapsed and died at an Internet cafe in the south-western city of Kwangju, after playing games non-stop for 86 hours and in August 2005, a 28-year-old identified only by his family name of Lee died while playing *StarCraft* for 50 hours non-stop at an internet cafe in the South Korean city of Taegu. Thankfully, such extreme cases are very much the exception.

Where South Korea leads, the rest of the world will undoubtedly follow. Online gaming is now the second-fastest growing gaming category in Europe and the USA and the worldwide market for online games is predicted to reach $9.8bn in 2009. PC gaming is still very much the cutting edge of online gaming, but with the introduction of Microsoft's online service "Xbox Live!" and the Sony PlayStation 3's networked gaming capability, console gamers are now rapidly adopting it, which means that it will inevitably move from hardcore to mainstream.

Indeed, in an echo of the real-world trade spawned by *Lineage*, we are now seeing virtual goods traded regularly for real-world cash on a number of online sites. For example, time-rich cash-poor gamers, such as students and the unemployed, are nurturing the skills and capabilities of in-game avatars, which they can then sell to other gamers who want to play a game at a high level but don't have the time to develop an avatar that will allow them to do so. It's also possible to trade in all manner of other virtual-world commodities, from magic spells to tools, from weapons to real estate. In fact, brokers are now emerging who specialize in trading in nothing else but virtual commodities such as these.

Edward Castronova, an associate professor of economics at California State University, completed a study of the economic activity surrounding the popular online role-playing game, *EverQuest*. He concluded that the *EverQuest* setting of Norrath enjoys a gross national product per capita of $2266 (bigger than China and India) – making it the 77th richest country in the world, ranking between Russia and Bulgaria!

Although some of the ramifications of online gaming are so bizarre they sound as if they come from another planet, the vast majority of online gamers at the moment – even in South Korea – remain firmly tethered to one fixed spot on Earth thanks to their dependency on a broadband landline connection. However, all this could change very soon. For gamers who feel the urge to ramble as they play, an answer is at hand. A new technology called "wi-fi" is now commonly available and offers wireless broadband connectivity to users wherever they are in a wi-fi-enabled area. This effectively blurs the distinction between fixed and wireless connections and allows gamers to play against opponents in real time wherever they are while on the move. Wi-fi is not yet truly mainstream in the West, with the USA hoping to reach a total of 32,800 commercial hotspots by the end of 2005, and the whole of Europe aiming for just 39,000. South Korea, however, currently accounts for almost half the world's hotspots, and its adoption of the latest WiBro technology (known as WiMax in the West) means that the newest hotspots will have a range of some 10km, making coverage of an entire town at one fell swoop a reality. So if you're waiting for a train in Pusan or killing time somewhere in a suburb of Seoul over a cup of coffee, instead of daydreaming or flicking through a magazine, you can log on to the Internet and jump into an online game – challenge a friend to a quick blast of *FIFA*, or drop into your favorite MMORPG to guide your avatar to glorious feats in its persistent virtual world. Does that sound seductive? Certainly this is why both Sony and Nintendo have bundled wi-fi technology in their latest handheld games platforms: the PSP (PlayStation Portable) and DS (Dual Screen) respectively.

Mobile gaming

Although wi-fi is spreading rapidly in the West, most mobile gaming is still single-player yet it is already the fastest growing entertainment category in Europe and the recent inclusion of mobile phone games in the best-sellers charts is a clear indication of the rapidly increasing take-up of downloadable games. At the moment, for most people, getting a game on a mobile means choosing from a list of available titles and then downloading through a WAP connection. Unfortunately, this can be slow and relatively costly. The continuing adoption of 3G technology should speed things up somewhat and it also seems likely that in the future, service providers will offer games for one-off or 24-hour usage, with one-off payments of as little as 10 cents.

Handset manufacturers are also alive to the opportunities. The Finnish giant Nokia has already embarked on a twin offensive: to provide phones that are truly capable gaming platforms, like the new N-Series devices, and to offer a gaming platform which is also a phone, in this case, the N-Gage. Although the N-Gage has only had a modest success – probably partly due to the limitations of the gaming experience and partly because it looks strange when used as a phone – Nokia is certainly ahead of the game at the moment. Crucially, its priorities are reflected by network coding companies; Ideaworks3D (long established in N-Gage circles) has already announced a partnership with Digital Bridges to bring its Airplay 2.0 multi-player framework to mobile games on the Series 60 handsets.

The British company Gizmondo is a new entrant in the field, with a device which works as a gaming platform as well as being a phone, a camera, a PDA, a camcorder, an MP3 player, and a

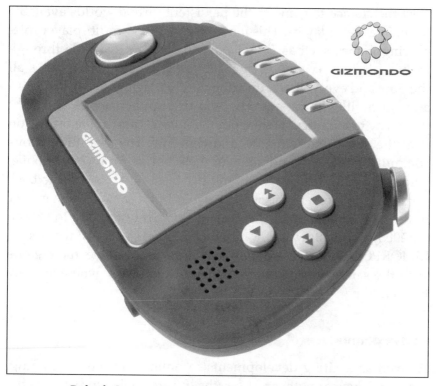

Britain's answer to the PlayStation Portable

global positioning system (GPS). The Gizmondo not only offers more gizmos than any comparable device, it is also innovating by offering GPS-based games that will send players to different locations in towns and cities, hopefully enabling players to bump into each other as they play and so creating new communities. Its pricing model is also interesting in that it charges a standard monthly fee for a service that carries advertising, but also offers an ad-free service at a higher rate. This could be a forerunner of what is to come – or, of course, it could go the way of Betamax in the videotape wars of the 1970s and early 1980s. Certainly, the Gizmondo management are nothing if not confident. There is a rumor that the center-piece of the Gizmondo boardroom is a real Scud missile with the words PlayStation painted on one side and Xbox on the other!

True wireless connectivity between handsets will no doubt give rise to a raft of exciting new possibilities in mobile gaming, not least the chance to game in the persistent virtual worlds available to static-access players. This means that massive multi-player role-playing games such as *EverQuest* will soon be available through mobile phone servers – giving gamers access to their avatars all the time and everywhere. Imagine you're playing the latest action-adventure title. In the morning you fire up the console and fight your way to a particular save point. At lunchtime in the office you load the game onto your PC and continue. Then, on the tedious commute home you pursue your adventures on your mobile, before finishing the day with another blast on your console back home. At the moment this isn't possible, but it can only be a matter of time. Technology currently in development (and due to launch in 2006) will allow both mobile and static-access worlds in MMORPGs to merge, enabling gamers to continue their game with the same avatars, but on different platforms, wherever they happen to be.

Active gaming

As well as exciting developments in online and mobile gaming, the third key growth area for the future looks sure to be the phenomenon that we have dubbed "active gaming." With people more pushed for time and more restricted for space than ever before and growing fears about personal safety in public spaces, there is a real need for health and fitness experiences that require the minimum of time and space. The rise of gym culture brought us the aerobics workout video in the 1980s and Pilates in the 1990s, but in the current decade it looks certain to be active gaming that fulfils that role.

Sportswear giants Reebok and Nike have already spotted active gaming's potential for health and fitness activities. Reebok have successfully launched their *CyberRider* and more recently *Cyberfit*, essentially an exercise bike with PlayStation controls attached to the handlebars. This gives you the chance to play your favorite game as you pedal away – certainly an improvement on watching a chat show on telly or zoning out with your iPod. But the clever thing with the *CyberRider* is the way the bike's flywheel is linked to the experience, because the faster you pedal, the faster the action on the

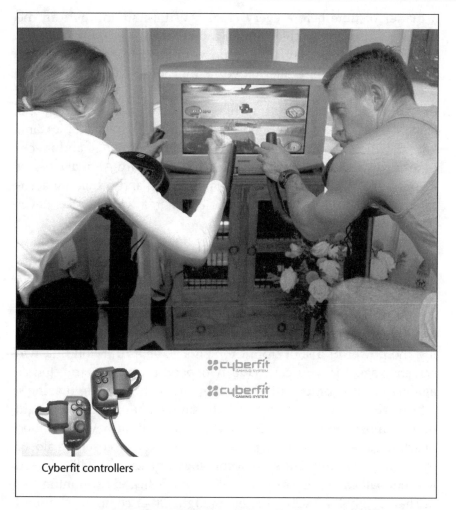

Cyberfit controllers

Reebok enters active gaming with its *Cyberfit*

screen takes place. So if, for example, you are playing the *FIFA* soccer game and your player has the ball, you can zip past a defender simply by pedaling more quickly. In the same way, if you are playing a driving game, a spurt on the bike will make your car accelerate away from your competitors. The result is that a change of pace and a spur of motivation are injected into what might otherwise be a fairly predictable ride. Especially since *CyberRider* technology has now been adapted to work with a whole range of other exercise machines in the new *Cyberfit* range, it now seems only a matter of time before every single health club and gym in the world is fitted with active gaming capabilities.

Meanwhile, Nike have linked up with Sony to produce *EyeToy: Kinetic*, a step-change alternative to the home workout video. It involves a series of exercises, all targeting different aspects of well-being. Some are aimed at improving fitness by taking moves and stances from tae kwon do, modern dance, kickboxing, aerobics, and karate. Others are less strenuous, borrowing from yoga and tai chi to focus on breathing, concentration, and flexibility. All make use of *EyeToy*'s interactive technology by monitoring and providing accurate feedback on the player's performance in a way that has never before been possible.

An interesting Korean innovation is a system that allows you to play table tennis against a computer. The player uses a real bat and is given the convincing impression that he or she is using a real ball, too. The technology is based on a similar principle to the *EyeToy* and uses a camera to register the player's movements, but it is so subtle and sensitive that it is able to pick up the nuances of spin as well as capturing the power of a shot from drop shot to smash. If you link two screens together, you can have two people playing table tennis against each other, even though they are standing side by side – which is a fairly surreal spectacle! The product has not been brought to the mainstream market yet, but it is typical of the new generation of active games in that it can be used as a workout, a coaching aid, or even just a bit of fun! The same technology can also be easily adapted to other ball games like tennis, squash, baseball, and badminton.

That is only the start of things, though. Other companies around the world are already working on games that combine this kind of camera technology with a dance mat, which adds the player's foot movements into the mix. This is enabling the development of very realistic and highly active soccer and other kicking games, as well as beat 'em ups and karate.

But perhaps the most exciting of all the active gaming prototypes currently under development is *Game Track*. This technology projects a three-meter cube around the gamer and monitors every single move of every part of the body within this space. It is easy to see how this would work as a more sophisticated version of the active sports games described above (a simple golf simulation using this

Nike enters the active gaming arena with *Motionworks*

technology has already been launched), but perhaps more exciting is the way that it might enable an entirely new interface with other game genres. So, for example, if you were playing an MMOFPS (massively multi-player online first-person shooter) and found yourself surrounded by enemies in the jungle, you would be able to creep through the undergrowth by moving your feet in the appropriate manner. Then you might part a fringe of leaves with your fingertips to identify the back of an enemy's head. Next, you lift your gun into the firing position and squeeze the trigger for the kill. From the outside you would look like a Jacques Lecoq mime artist performing a series of elaborate moves on the spot, but for the player himself, it would be an experience so utterly immersive and thrilling that it would feel just like the real thing ... or maybe even better, because if things really got too hot for you, you could always walk away, dial up a pizza, and grab a beer from the fridge.

Professional gaming

At the top end of the gaming community are the professional gamers: men and women who live and breath gaming, playing either solo or in teams, known as "clans." In fact, many of them do not consider themselves to be gamers at all, but serious athletes. And why shouldn't they? In the highly competitive and extremely lucrative world of cyber-athletics, competitors follow training regimes every bit as punishing as their non-cyber cousins: they exercise to keep physically and mentally fit, follow strict diets, and put in endless hours of practice.

Leading the way in pro gaming is the networked first-person shooter *Counter-Strike* – the world's most popular online game – which is now played for seriously high stakes. Professional *Counter-Strike* clans compete in global gaming leagues and in tournaments with prize money in excess of $1 million. These attract large crowds of spectators at the venue itself, with many more watching live online. They are also followed by fans who can download highlights from the Internet or watch on specialist TV programs.

Already, the top clans like SK Gaming from Sweden have achieved global fame within the gaming community, and some have even launched their own brands of gaming peripherals and clothing. Visit the SK Gaming website and you have the chance to buy SK-branded gear like gaming gloves specially designed for "less friction between hand and mousepad" or a steel grip to "reduce sweat problems." Indeed, some pro gamers are beginning to enjoy the same sort of fame and success enjoyed by non-cyber sportspeople. Johnathan Wendel, better known by his gaming alias Fatal1ty, has won six Cyberathlete Professional World champion- ships, enjoys superstar status, and has struck a deal with Creative Labs to design gaming peripherals and accessories to be sold under the Fatal1ty name.

Most pro gamers and clans will use gaming aliases or "handles" like Fatal1ty or SK Gaming, which has the lucky side effect of enabling them to market themselves as brands far more effectively. In much the same way as the name of a soccer team – Arsenal or Juven- tus – will outlive even its biggest stars, so these gaming handles have the potential to become brands that will outlast the gamers to whom they first belonged.

Hooking up with a gaming brand like SK Gaming or Fatal1ty offers a fantastic gateway into the gaming arena. Many of the top clans already have sponsorship deals with leading brands although to date these have been mainly in the technology sector where the fit is both natural and obvious. The growth of the pro gaming scene, however, means it can only be a matter of time before big non-tech consumer lifestyle brands join the fray, and it is quite conceivable that in ten years' time the top gaming clans will be well on the way to becoming as famous and as valuable – in every sense – as the top football teams are today. Sounds unlikely? Then remember that ten years ago there was no pro gaming scene at all. In fact, no networked gaming to speak of, and definitely no big money global gaming tournaments. These days the Samsung-sponsored World Cyber Games (WCG) is a fixture on the international sporting calendar. In 2005, around 1.2 million hopefuls entered their national WCG qualifiers, with some 800 gamers from around 70 countries advancing to the Grand Finals in Singapore, where they were accommodated in a special Players' Village – just like their counterparts in the Olympics! For 2006 the WCG is coming to Europe for the first time, bringing the biggest global event in gaming to the Italian city of Monza.

Augmented-reality gaming

Some of the ideas at the leading edge of games development are quite mind-boggling. One idea which certainly takes some getting used to is augmented-reality gaming (ARG). ARG uses the real world as a gaming space and invites its players to pursue their gaming objectives through the buildings and streets of real towns and cities. It works by merging different technologies such as GPS, Bluetooth, virtual reality, wi-fi, infrared, and sensing mechanisms to create a system that allows gamers to play in a digitally-enhanced maze-like version of the real world.

Following the success of *PacManhattan*, a real-life version of the classic arcade game in which the streets of New York were turned into a gaming arena for students with GPS-enabled handsets, researchers in Singapore are now developing an augmented-reality version which superimposes the virtual 3D game world onto the city streets and buildings. Players equipped with a wearable computer, headset, and goggles physically enter a real-world game space by choosing to play the role of Pacman or one of the Ghosts. The human Pacman "sees" virtual cookies scattered on the street, which the player can then "eat" by walking through them. Ghosts

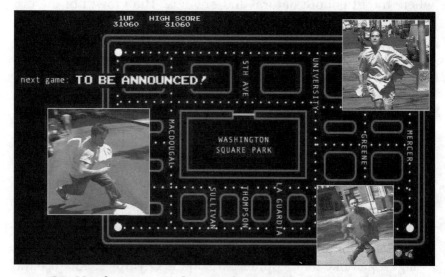

PacManhattan: **students take gaming to the streets in New York**

get to "devour" a player whom they catch up with in the game area by tapping him or her on the shoulder. In return, Pacman gets the ability to temporarily neutralize them and acquire new virtual powers by finding and picking up Bluetooth-embedded physical sugar jars scattered in the real world environment by a game co-ordinator. The players' locations are also wirelessly updated to a virtual 3D Pac-world where online gamers can view their progress and participate by helping either Pacman or the Ghosts through text messaging.

Elsewhere, the University of Southern Australia has developed an ARG version of the *Quake* game, and plans to launch ARG engines into the market with a target price tag of AU$500 by the end of 2006. It looks likely that ARG technology will be a key driver in the active gaming arena over the next two to five years.

Conclusion: watch this space

With technology giants like Sony and Microsoft gearing up for battle and games developers scrambling to entertain ever more demanding and hungry consumers, resources are already pouring into the games industry. As they do so, the pace of development will accelerate and the possibilities will become ever more extraordinary. Indeed, some of the wilder gaming ideas in this chapter will no doubt soon be remarkably commonplace. Because, there's no doubt about it, the games rush is on and those that fail to catch a ride on this tailgate are going to see it whistle over the far horizon.

CHAPTER 7

Morphing giants

How the gaming industry will evolve

The value chain

The sums of money involved in the gaming industry are awesome. You can get a feel for it from a quick back-of-the-envelope calculation. At the moment, a publisher like Electronic Arts might reckon to sell about 10 million copies of a top game title, which would retail at roughly $40 per copy. So at retail, that one title might generate $400 million globally. With gaming growing as strongly as it is now, it's not unreasonable to suggest that in three years' time a top title might sell as many as 25 million copies: in other words, a single game title could generate a cool $1 billion!

That revenue is currently shared out along a value chain, such as the one for a computer game, shown in Figure 7.1. Despite all the technical wizardry that the gaming industry employs, the business is still basically about shipping discs in boxes – and, as this is a young industry operating on a global scale, it's no surprise that the distributor and retailer capture quite a lot of the value in the chain. So, for a typical PC game title, around 60 percent of the value might be shared between the developer (who creates the games and designs the programs) and the publisher (who takes responsibility for production and controls distribution). Since many publishers will have no direct access to retail channels, a distributor may take roughly 10 percent of the value for organizing this part of the process, with the retailer getting around 30 percent for getting it to the end user. However, it seems highly probable that as the industry evolves, steps will be taken to reduce the complexity of the chain, in particular by cutting back the number of "middle men" between developer and consumer.

Figure 7.1

Industry structure

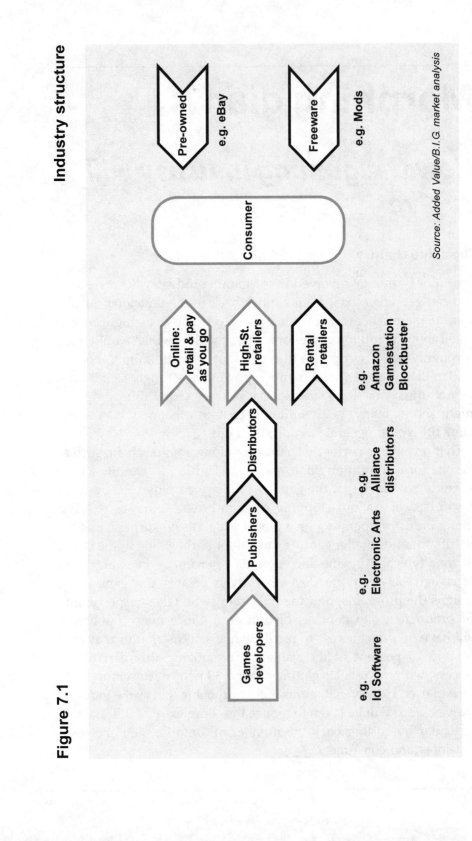

Source: Added Value/B.I.G. market analysis

We'll look at some of the emerging new channels and business models that will facilitate these developments a bit later in the chapter, but first let's review the state of play for some of the key figures in the chain.

The developers

These days, developing a new computer game is a seriously time-consuming and costly business, with the big studios operating on a similarly grand scale to their Hollywood cousins. During the development process, a top publisher like Electronic Arts may bring together hundreds of people: programmers, technical experts (for disciplines such as motion capture), specialist consultants (such as racing drivers, military experts, or engineers), animators, and music composers, to name but a few – all working to a multi-million dollar budget over a period of perhaps several years. *Half-Life* 2, the eagerly anticipated sequel to one of the most acclaimed games of all time, took five years and more than $40 million to develop. Indeed, in the UK, the Bafta awards now include several categories for computer games; could it be that their US counterpart, the Oscars, will soon be following suit?

Just a few years ago, video game design was largely a cottage industry and, amazingly, in an industry that now dwarfs Hollywood, there is still room for the lone developer: someone with a unique idea and the tenacity to take on the established industry giants. One such example is Chris Sawyer, the man behind the hugely successful *RollerCoaster Tycoon* series, who was driven by a desire to create a fun but non-violent game – and to make a little money along the way. And happily, he was successful on all counts!

Perhaps even more incredible is the continued existence of "bedroom coders": the dedicated (and talented) amateurs who devote their spare time to game programming. So how is this possible? The answer is that the giant studios and the little guys have learnt to work together in mutually beneficial ways.

One of the best examples of this is the phenomenon of modifying – or "mod'ing" – an existing game which is the property of someone else, usually one of the giant studios. This was the way in which the most popular of all online networked games, the first-person

Five years and $40 million to develop

shooter (FPS) *Counter-Strike* came into being. This mod was adapted from the single player FPS *Half-Life* and was created by a multi-national alliance of bedroom coders who shared a single common goal: to take the best-ever FPS and turn it from a single-player experience into a multi-player spectacular, which they did, with astounding success. Soon *Counter-Strike* was being hailed as the best game ever (today it forms the backbone of many pro gaming tournaments) – and it was made available online, absolutely free. So how do the games developer and publisher benefit from this? First of all, it drives sales, as the mod requires the original game to run it. It also extends the life of the game and keeps it at the front of gamers' minds, while building top-end equity among the gaming community and helping to recruit new developer talent.

To their credit, both developers and publishers have been quick to realize the huge and largely untapped potential of mod'ers, and many actively offer "dev kits" (development kits, containing all the necessary paraphernalia for mod'ing) free of charge – indeed, these often ship with the game. They are also quick to snap up the best talent when it emerges. So the publishers make more money and the erstwhile amateur and bedroom coders become salaried programmers united under one roof. The mod'ing community benefits through seeing its heroes elevated to lead programmers in top studios. The studios get to keep the talent while providing the resources to give the code the polish it deserves. And it means there's more room for new bedroom coding talent to emerge (suitably incentivized). So it's a win–win situation for all concerned. In fact, one of the main reasons a game like *Quake* is still going strong over a decade after its first release in 1995 is the fact that people are still happy to create and play mods for it.

But wait – it's not only the bedroom coders who are ceding control to the publishers. Developers are too, and not only the small studios. Recent moves by the larger publishers and platform owners have seen takeovers and buy-outs of sizeable development studios, giving the publishers and platform owners greater control of the content produced and a tighter grip on the budget and timelines. Oh, and they also make more money. Which is nice for them.

Perhaps the best recent example of this was Microsoft's takeover of developers Bungie, who were developing a PC game called *Halo*.

Mr Gates knew that for the Xbox to succeed he would need a killer title, a must-have that was exclusive to his new toy, and *Halo* was a perfect fit. As it was already eagerly anticipated by the gaming community, Microsoft took the calculated risk of upsetting PC gamers by securing the rights to *Halo* as an Xbox exclusive for its first six months of release. But Bungie were shrewd. They didn't want to sell the rights to just one game: they knew this was their chance to sell their golden goose. So Microsoft were persuaded to buy the studio lock, stock, and barrel, not only giving themselves a great game and all its future derivatives but also guaranteeing sales of their new platform, while Bungie were kept happy with bundles and bundles of cash. Indeed, for all concerned, nothing was better than the sight of Bungie jumping!

The publishers

Currently there are 12 main players in the first tier of games publishers (in addition to the major platform owners who also publish some titles themselves), who between them account for the vast majority of all the AAA (pronounced "triple A" – best-selling) titles published. All of these publishers come from North America, Europe, or Japan and many – such as Electronic Arts, Eidos, Vivendi, Atari, and Sega – are now themselves household names. As well as these, there are a number of second-tier publishers who account for a good number of popular franchises, although their inability to compete with the massive marketing budgets of the big 12 mean the titles in their portfolios might not be so well known outside gaming communities. A full list of first and second-tier games publishers can be found in Appendix 2 on page 141.

There are also a great many smaller, often specialized, publishers, such as Just Flight (flight simulators and specialist add-on packs for photo-realistic scenery, virtual communications with the control tower etc.) and Arxel Tribe (action/adventure games). And there is a healthy line in second-phase games publishing, with brands such as Sold Out and Platinum leading the charge. Their speciality is re-publishing titles once their initial purple patch has waned (typically 6–12 months), in a no-frills format (simple CD/DVD case replacing fancy box packaging, instruction manual replaced by PDF file) and at a greatly reduced price. After a period of, typically, 6–9 months in this state they may then be re-released once more at an even cheaper price, often as low as $10. Little wonder then that the big players don't want to get involved in this end of the market, preferring instead to pass their games on to the bargain-basement specialists.

But there's no doubt about it: the elephant at the publishing picnic is Electronic Arts. EA are not just the biggest games publisher on the planet, they are one of the world's biggest entertainment companies. Period. They own some of the biggest-selling and best-known games properties, which they publish under three brand names: EA, EA SPORTS™, and EA SPORTS BIG™. Around a third of these games, like *The Sims, SSX*, and *Need For Speed* are wholly EA-owned, while the other two-thirds, including *FIFA* and *Harry Potter*, are published under license.

Electronic Arts' key brand portfolio

When we talked to Andrew Corcoran, EA's European Director for Strategic Planning, he referred to their games as "intellectual properties" (IPs) rather than brands in themselves, aligning them with EA's other IPs, which extend beyond the titles, and allowing them to hunt down anything that can make their games unique, which could be a character or the world characters inhabit or even a special move that has never been seen before. Undoubtedly

The Sims could be run as a separate company – a brand in its own right, with individual, pre-determined, and named characters spinning out of the main game much as the TV series *Frasier* span out from *Cheers* – but it would appear that EA are much more intent on focusing on quality and product features than on brand-building per se. EA's aim is always to develop the best possible game, rather than producing something that will appeal to a particular group or building a mega property that they can leverage. As Andrew Corcoran told us:

> *"Through mega games, we get mega properties."*

In this, their approach is reminiscent of marketeers of fast moving consumer goods (FMCGs) in the 1970s and 1980s, a time when product features and quality were key differentiators. As these became commoditized, so the FMCG focus shifted onto mega-properties and branding. It seems likely that, as games publishing matures and excellent quality and product features are taken for granted by all, so brands will become similarly important. And any marketeer's mouth must be watering at the prospect. Just imagine, as you wend your way up the drive to EA's HQ in Redwood, California, you pass numerous life-size (or bigger!) characters from EA's considerable portfolio of games peering out at you through the trees. The comparison with Disney is there for anyone to make ... so how long will it be before we see the first EA theme park?

Which is not to say that EA are unaware of the opportunities they are generating: it is perhaps just that there are too many of them to address all at once! Certainly, EA are as aware as everyone else that eyeballs are moving away from TV, and that gaming offers a fantastic alternative. However, finding a way of getting brands into the gameplay is no easy matter, as we saw in Chapter 3. From the perspective of a publisher like EA, one of the biggest problems is global long-term scalability. Many of the brands which understand the opportunities gaming presents are young brands that don't yet have a global reach or the financial muscle to work effectively in such a big arena – which suggests that the bigger your brand, the easier it should be to get into gaming.

Another factor holding brands back from gaming is the advertising agencies themselves, who don't have expertise in this field and so are steering their clients towards TV and billboards in the time-honored fashion. However, this is starting to change. There are now some specialist media agencies with the technology to serve ads into online games in real time, although the big global agencies are still lagging behind in this area. No doubt at a certain point in the not too distant future, they will wake up to the opportunities and when they do, you can be certain that the big beasts among the games publishers will be licking their lips!

The retailers

Let's be honest. In this business, the retailers' days are numbered. No point dwelling here, then. Next!. ... Well, actually, it may not be quite as simple as that. Today's computer and video games retailers are not only alive and well, they are positively thriving. Currently, there are seven main retail streams: high-street specialist games chain stores, high-street independent specialist games stores, high-street entertainment stores, multiples, e-retail, rental outlets and resellers. Quite a list, but that's hardly surprising given the size of the industry and the fact that it plugs directly into the heart of future retail consumerism.

The high-street specialist gaming chain stores are companies like GAME in the UK and Gamestation and Electronics Boutique in the USA, which focus exclusively on the retail of all things to do with computer and video gaming: software, hardware, associated peripherals, fashion accessories, strategy guide books, and so on. Such stores have mushroomed in recent years, attracting a devoted consumer base: when GAME in the UK launched its loyalty card, five million people signed up in the first year!

At the moment stores such as these are clearly different from entertainment stores like Virgin, but we are pretty sure that the distinction between them will start to blur. Already a store like Virgin dedicates around a third of its retail space to gaming, and that proportion is growing all the time at the expense of music and DVD/video. In the meantime, as in-game soundtracks become ever more popular (some, such as those for *Grand Theft Auto: San Andreas* and the *Final Fantasy* series are even released as albums in their own right), how long will it be before the gaming specialists start selling music too?

The big multiples like Tesco, Carrefour, and Wal-Mart are also getting in on the act. In fact Tesco has found that in an astonishingly short period of time, gaming has come from nowhere to be one of its fastest growing categories. With results like that, how long will it be until the multiples start selling consoles and PCs as well?

There are also still a number of independent games specialist retailers who remain a significant force – for now, at least. However, it seems highly likely that these will be forced into niche positions by the big players, much as happened to the small independent record stores in the past.

Online, games are sold through the usual suspects like Amazon, as well as specialists such as GAME who are incentivizing people to buy through this channel by offering lower prices.

Games rental is also booming, with chains like Blockbuster stocking games alongside DVDs. The games publishers seem to be relaxed about this, as they see many gamers renting on a "try before you buy" basis. It's also likely that online rental will grow, with the development of technology that allows games to be downloaded from the Internet and then unlocked for a set period.

We are also seeing a lot of action in the reselling markets, with the likes of Amazon and eBay doing brisk business with people who want to "play it and trade it."

All these kinds of games retailers are riding the gaming wave at the moment, but we have no doubt that over the next few years, this part of the gaming value chain will see some dramatic changes, as we'll find out next.

New business models and channels

With so much happening in the gaming world, picking tomorrow's winners can be a mug's game. But we're going to stick our necks out and look at three new business models which look well-placed to shake up the industry: the Steam download technology pioneered by Valve, the South Korean firm Nexon's *Kart Rider* model, and EA's Pogo website.

Let's start with Steam and a small developer called Valve. Once upon a time they produced a game called *Half-Life* which everyone thought would be a very good, if rather obvious, first-person shooter. But it wasn't. It was, quite simply, the best game anyone had ever written. In *Half-Life*, for the very first time, players could immerse themselves in the game without ever needing to leave it – all the narrative, all the information the player needed in order to progress was given in the game itself, by the game's characters. Unsurprisingly it became a number-one selling AAA title overnight and went on to spawn the equally popular *Counter-Strike*. At a stroke, Valve's fame in the industry was assured. However, they didn't want to rest on their laurels and decided to take a huge risk. They put all their eggs in one basket and ploughed every cent they had made on *Half-Life* into developing its sequel. They estimated it would take them four years, although it ended up taking five because some of the source code was leaked on the Net and the FBI had to be called in to catch the miscreants – but that's another story! Anyway, as you might expect, there was no shortage of offers from the big publishers to buy Valve, but they ignored them all, and it soon became very apparent why. Far from wanting to cede control to the publishers, Valve intended to bypass them altogether.

It turned out that in those five years, Valve had been developing not just *Half-Life 2*, but also a means of distributing the game without the need for a publisher. The new distribution method was simple: make it downloadable from the net. So why hadn't everyone thought of doing it? Well, they probably had, but while the idea was simple, its implementation was hellishly difficult. For a start, it would need more code than could be burnt onto a rack of CDs and there were also major headaches over security. But, amazingly, Valve cracked it and they announced their new download service, Steam, with the launch of *Half-Life 2*. PC owners were given the option of using it right away as a way of purchasing the new game and were rewarded if they did so. Although the download takes several hours, the packets of data are downloaded in advance of the game's release date, usually overnight, and then sit dormant on the gamer's computer until activated at midnight on the given day. An elegant solution to what had once seemed an intractable problem!

But it's in the future that Valve intend to make their money, both by using Steam themselves and by licensing the technology to other developers – and to publishers too, if they want to pay for it. Indeed, *Half-Life 3* will almost certainly only be available through downloads. And with the continued roll-out and take-up of broadband, and with the next-generation consoles able to take advantage of such technology, Steam seems set to be the future of content distribution. But if the developers will be using it, and publishers too can take advantage of it (for a price), who will be the real losers? Well, it looks like that might well be the end-of-line vendors, both e-retailers and high-street shops.

But this type of technology is not the only threat to the established order. The South Korean company, Nexon Corp, have developed an entirely new model of making money from online games, with phenomenal success: in 2004, their revenues were $110 million, rising to $250 million in 2005. The basis of their success is an online racing game called *Kart Rider*, launched in 2004. Nexon says that over 12 million people – a quarter of the South Korean population – have participated in a *Kart Rider* race, and at any one time there may be as many as 200,000 players racing against each other online.

The really clever part, though, is how Nexon makes its money from it. Normally, online gaming companies charge their users a subscription to play in the virtual online world they have created. Nexon, however, allows anyone to race for free and makes its money from selling more upmarket cars and accessories. So you can pimp your ride with a $1 paint job or buy a special pair of goggles to see through digital smoke for $3.50 or, if you're feeling really flush, why not splash out $9.80 on a top-of-the-range vehicle with far superior handling? It means that players form a close personal bond with the game, as it allows them to express their individuality

and take real pride in their car and avatar. It also enables players to choose their level of expenditure, making it accessible to kids who want to play with their pocket money as well as to wealthy young professionals who want to indulge themselves. In fact, the game is already attracting dedicated professionals backed by local sponsors who race in tournaments offering prize money of over $50,000 supplied by companies such as Coca-Cola.

The widespread adoption of broadband, combined with compelling online games, looks sure to attract more and more gamers online. And with innovative business models such as Nexon's able to leverage their commercial potential, the middle men in the value chain are once again likely to feel the pressure.

Unsurprisingly, Electronic Arts have been alive to the potential of online gaming for quite some time, and now have a website called Pogo.com that offers simple, quick multi-player games such as hearts, checkers, mahjong, and solitaire. Just like Nexon's *Kart Rider*, access to the games is free, but in this case EA make their money from advertising which appears regularly and prominently on the site. And for advertisers, Pogo is certainly a tempting prospect. EA estimate that they already have around 14 million unique users every month, playing for an average of an hour per session for up to 17 hours a week. Players are attracted not just by the compulsive nature of the games themselves, but also by the chance of winning cash prizes: as they play, they collect points which they can then spend on raffle tickets for entry into prize draws. They also have the chance, after every successful game, to win the ever-increasing jack-pot shown on screen. And they can hook up with friends, or make new ones, in the chatrooms. Pogo's appeal is targeted directly at the Quick fun and play gamer – the retired person or housewife, perhaps, seeking a break from routine or relief from boredom. In the past, they might have flicked on daytime TV; in the future, they will be far more likely to go online and game, pausing occasionally to click through to a company website whose link has just popped up on the screen in front of them. And with Pogo To Go rolling out for the mobile market, EA look set to consolidate their dominant position in this market still further.

Conclusion

There is no industry better placed than gaming to take advantage of leading edge developments in online distribution. After all, its products are essentially weightless and its consumers are among the most tech-savvy people on the planet. The future certainly looks glum for bricks-and-mortar games retailers, however rosy things might seem at the moment. As these traditional middle men are squeezed by the moves to online gaming and online retail, real power and influence will be increasingly concentrated at the top end of the gaming value chain, with canny developers finding ingenious new ways to market, and the biggest publishers and hardware manufacturers entrenching their power. Companies like these already have an acute understanding of the role that non-gaming brands can play in their business and – as EA's success with Pogo shows – are actively seeking ways of bringing brands into the gaming arena. So, next let's look in more detail at the practical steps you can take to ensure that your brand makes the most of these extraordinary opportunities.

CHAPTER 8

Press "start" to play

Leveraging gaming for your brand

Developing a vision

We hope that by now we have convinced you that it is time to stop sitting on your hands and to get off the bench and enter the gaming arena with your brand. But what are the first practical steps that need to be taken?

Right from the start, it is essential that you develop a vision of what you want to achieve through your involvement in gaming. Who are your target consumers? What is their relationship with gaming? What are the key insights that connect them to gaming? The answers might lead you to formulate a very simple, short-term objective like "to achieve brand-awareness among a new target group." Or, it might be more strategic and long term, such as "to build a 21st-century globally-scaled leveragable marketing asset for our brand across all markets, that opens up new audiences, new media, and new routes to market." Whichever way you choose to do it, you should put the consumer at the heart of your vision, and whatever you hope to achieve, it is crucial that you are clear about your intentions.

Next, look at where in your mix gaming can deliver most effectively and ensure that gaming is properly integrated with your brand objectives. This is an obvious exercise, but a useful one in our experience, as gaming may well be able to deliver in more ways than at first seem obvious. Its multi-dimensional nature – providing a new media channel and a new media vehicle, as well as offering a new audience and a new sales channel – means it may present longer term opportunities that stretch way beyond the initial targets you are setting. So, consider formulating a multiple-horizon vision, where, for example, the first horizon is about new audiences and a new media channel, with the second horizon being about new marketing properties and the third, new routes to market.

Finally, create clear key performance indicators (KPIs) by which to measure yourself. It is especially important to do this in any new area, so that everyone involved knows which targets to shoot for when faced with new issues and choices.

Protocols

As we saw in Chapter 3, it is vital to remember that gaming is a completely new media with its own codes and practices, its own private language and protocols. At a first glance, it might look similar to movies; after all, it has a similar global scale and reach, some of its themes are similar and some of its audiences overlap – but don't be fooled. Gaming, let us repeat, is unlike any other media you will have dealt with before.

So over the portal to the gaming arena, engrave the following Dos and Don'ts:

DO stay out of the game itself ... unless you feel your brand will be perceived as real and credible in that particular context.	**DON'T** do your own content ... unless it is right at the cutting edge and you are certain that it will blow people away.
DO use your size and power to do something that only you can do ... if you have the scale to do something really impressive then that's exactly what your consumers will be expecting of you.	**DON'T** just jump into bed with anyone ... certain gaming brands hold far more sway than others, so take advice from someone who really understands the industry.

Although gaming dangles the potential of access to a genuinely global market, beware of treating that market as homogenous. Even though computer gaming has a dominant language (US English) and straddles cultures and countries far more comfortably than

Figure 8.1

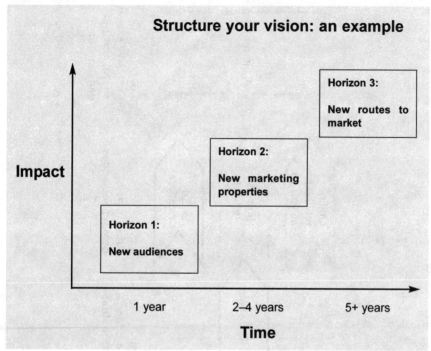

Structure your vision: an example

many other media, you will still find major differences. In Europe, you just have to look at the differing penetrations of broadband between Italy and Denmark, or the differences in the popularity of game genres between countries (UK, first-person shooters; France, adventure; Germany, strategy) to appreciate how complicated things can be. This does not mean there are not many opportunities for pan-European marketing activities, it just means that the nuts and bolts have to be thought through with the teams on the ground in each country. So, when looking for leverageable assets, first make sure they really are big in each market you are intending to target.

Key areas of opportunity

So, where exactly in the gaming value chain can you leverage your brand most effectively? To work this out, you need to consider your own brand's value chain from the point of view of gaming. Look at what assets you possess and how they could add value for gaming partners.

Figure 8.2

**The gaming chain:
where can your brand add value?**

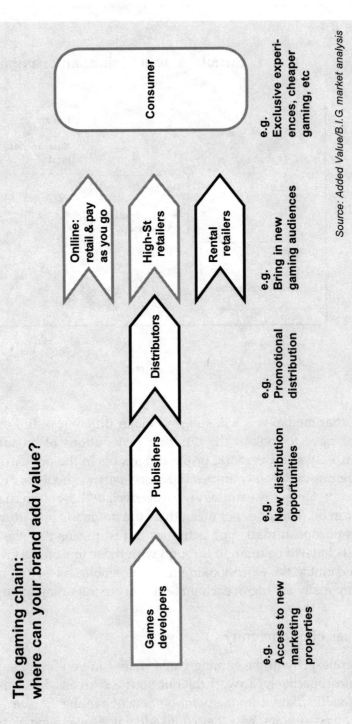

Source: Added Value/B.I.G. market analysis

If you have considerable expertise or credibility in a particular field, think about how this could be used to add credibility to a game. For example, Ford have been quick to capitalize on the success of driving games by lending their name and their products to the *Ford Racing* series, while brands already associated with soccer have leveraged this still further through sponsorship of the *FIFA* football game. So make sure that you own the gaming rights to any existing sports sponsorships that you may have, as they can be highly strategic and very valuable assets in the gaming arena. After all, where would EA's *PGA Tour* golf game be without Tiger Woods' endorsement? There are a great many sports games currently in development, so whatever your asset there may be a real opportunity to leverage it with a new audience via gaming. The Chairman's penchant for sailing may turn into your newest new media push!

You should also look at your own distribution channels and see if they might be of interest to potential gaming partners. The gaming industry is still at a relatively early stage of development, so it is quite possible that access to the scale and reach of your distribution channels could be extremely interesting for them. Do you have retail space to share? Can you share entertainment properties with them? Can you give publishers new channels to market? For example, they are always looking for new ways to get consumers to trial their games; could they use your channels to do this, with benefits to both sides? You might also think about joint promotions that lower price thresholds for consumers.

Games publishers are constantly seeking new ways of connecting with multiple audiences. So, if your brand delivers a significant share of a particular consumer segment or commands respect with hard-to-reach consumers it could be of great value to them. This is not just confined to youth brands; games publishers are looking to touch discerning 25–35 year olds, the influential and growing 55+ consumer base, as well as women, mothers, and many more.

Then, there are ways of reaching out to the gamers themselves. Could you help up-and-coming game developers to secure a publisher? Perhaps you could supply seed money for new talent to develop their games, in much the same way as brands support new talent in the film business? Or what about involvement with championship gaming? Have you thought of creating events and prizes or supporting individuals and teams?

Whatever strategy you are considering, you need to keep a weather eye on the potential implications of convergence in the gaming market. The pace of change is fierce, so we believe it is wise to consider the implications of this in your strategy – more so than in the far more stable and predictable world of film. The key convergences in gaming are happening in two areas: the consolidation of publishers/developers and platform convergence.

Electronic Arts is already the behemoth in the games publishing market and holds many (but not all) of the "triple A" titles that command the greatest sales. It is now eyeing up second-tier publishers with a view to increasing its dominance, while second-tier publishers in turn are swallowing up third-tier players in a bid to compete with EA. All this means that you have to think carefully about which publisher you want to start cutting your deals with.

Along with the much talked about convergence in the music/PC/TV area, there is also considerable convergence in gaming platforms. Most big titles are multi-platform; in other words, they are available across PC, Xbox, and PlayStation. The trend to multi-platform games will continue and advance into the mobile arena too, which is currently the biggest growth area. This means that the biggest titles will be playable on all significant platforms, which will greatly improve their reach and frequency. It is therefore vital that in seeking a game to work with you consider how platform-independent it is/will be. You should also think forward several years to a time when everyone has full gaming and Internet commerce capability on their mobiles. Where would you like your brand to be in this? What actions now would set this up?

Finally, think about how your brand's position in online gaming will interface with your other online assets such as your website and other micro sites. How do you want your brand to be perceived in the world of online commerce?

Who to target?

In deciding on the type of gamer to focus on, the first step is to look at the overlap between your core brand target and the gaming segments we have outlined: is there some direct correlation? You may need to do some simple research among your consumers to see

Figure 8.3

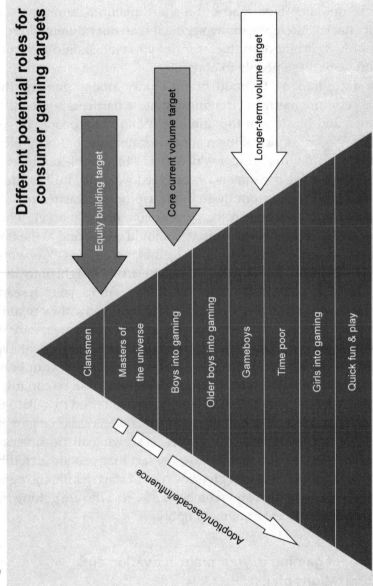

Different potential roles for consumer gaming targets

Equity building target

Core current volume target

Longer-term volume target

Clansmen

Masters of the universe

Boys into gaming

Older boys into gaming

Gameboys

Time poor

Girls into gaming

Quick fun & play

Adoption/cascade/influence

the penetration of gaming (Who games? What type of gaming – console, online, mobile? Which platform?), the occasions (When do they game? With whom? For how long?) and look for any correspondence with use of your product.

The second step is to map out a short, medium, and long-term plan of attack. Different gaming segments can offer different opportunities for your brand, so the activities you plan should reflect the role you want these people to play.

If you are looking to build brand equity among gamers, then there is certainly merit in targeting the more hardcore segments of Clansmen and Masters of the universe. What these people do and say filters down to the mainstream via chatrooms, industry press, and online forums, in a similar way to the fashion or hi-tech markets where leading edge consumers are targeted with the latest products to create pull-through from those in the aspiring mainstream.

To activate your brand in the current core of the market, where large-scale activity will bear fruit, you should be looking at the Boys into gaming and Older boys into gaming segments. We would strongly recommend that you gain some fresh insight into these segments with respect to your brand by getting your research people to set up some focus groups and explore how they relate to your market sector and your brand. Or to get a quick idea, why not log onto a chat forum for a major game and listen. You might even try asking a few simple questions, but direct probing on your brand will most probably get a short, unfavorable reply – so be careful!

For mainstream influence in the long term, you need to look to the real volume market, which at the moment is the occasional gamers' sector – but their involvement in gaming is growing all the time. So if you get a foothold into gaming now, the fact that you are a credible presence in this vast area will give you a head start in influencing the huge mainstream of men and women of all ages who are getting into gaming as a regular entertainment option.

The place of gaming in your main activation and communications plans

Just imagine being back at the start of the cinema and the possibilities that medium could have thrown up for brands willing to

Figure 8.4

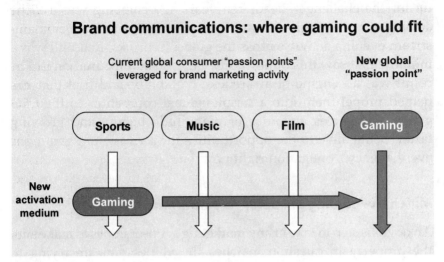

get involved. From a marketeer's point of view, gaming is the new film or football. It is both a new global consumer passion point and a new brand activation medium for existing passion points. It's as global as sport, as commercially savvy as film, and as digitally manipulable as music. We confidently expect that in five years' time most major brand owners will have gaming activation roles within their marketing organizations, just as they do for film and sport today.

Of course, marketeers know a lot about film and music and sport; they make it their business to know the ins and outs of the areas that their consumers spend so much time and money on. It's now high time to do the same with gaming. The truly different aspect to gaming as a new passion point is its ability to cut right across all existing consumer passion points as a new form of activation medium.

So, if you have a major association or sponsorship deal with a certain sport, look at gaming as a way of further leveraging the investment you have already made. You need to make sure that your activation agencies (Promotions, Direct marketing, PR, Events ... all disciplines) are up to speed on gaming and its possibilities. Do they know their MMORPG from their FPS? Could they set up a gaming event around your key asset in sport/music/film?

It's time to assess the capabilities you have around you and gear up for the challenge ahead. Ten years ago clubbing was a niche activity for seemingly deviant lifestyles; now it's a major mainstream evening activity across the globe. In drinks, Red Bull was a minnow that saw this opportunity early on and focused on it. The result was an engine of awareness, credibility, and trial that has helped propel them into a serious global competitor to the CSD giants. Gaming is an order of magnitude bigger, and growing faster. Being alive to the opportunities for activation in gaming is every agency's obligation right now.

Match the gaming property to your brand equity

An obvious step to take in any marketing sponsorship is to make sure the property in question matches the values you are trying to espouse. But you only have to look around you to see howling mismatches everywhere. Too often, marketeers assume too much of the property and too little of the intelligence of the average person. They simply collide their brand with some event or personality, cross their fingers, and hope that some "coolness" will just rub off.

Great tie-ups lie in sharing some fundamental values or equity between brand and property. Just think of Coca-Cola and the Olympics; they both share a belief in global positivity and unity, and that's why it works.

The first step is to be crystal clear about your current positioning (what makes you different, what people think you stand for) and brand character. Then be equally clear about where you want to get to – your desired brand positioning and character.

Experience has taught us that positioning is not a static place you attain, but an *idea* towards which you strive continually. Be clear where you want to be, and the line between where you are and this ideal spot is your trajectory.

The second step is to ask consumers. Never assume. Even if you and the gaming property owners agree on the marvelous synergies in equity and how positive your union will be – check it out. Only believe it when you hear ordinary people say it.

Lay out your brand equities clearly – the functional and emotional aspects of your brand that make it unique, and the reasons that consumers buy it.

Figure 8.5

	Equity matching	
	Your brand	**Potential gaming property**
Idea – The idea at the core, its essence or point of view on the world		☐
Character – personality traits; describe it as a person		☐
Benefits – functional – What do consumers get?		☐
Benefits – emotional – How does it make people feel?		☐
Visual equities – The core visual aspects that make it recogniza-ble (color, shape, logo, design elements, adv. property etc.)		☐
Heritage – Important or well known events, imagery, or claims from history		☐

10 = Good match   **0** = Bad match

Figure 8.5 gives you a simple framework to fill out. Fill it out for your brand in the second column and then repeat for the proposed equity in the third column. What you are looking for is some strong synergy in one or two places. This is then the foundation of your tie-up and where thinking should begin as to what activities you should embark on together.

The strategic options

Throughout the book we have alluded to and discussed ways in which branded businesses could leverage gaming as a potential marketing platform. Here we have mapped them on a scale showing the level of commitment required from you – the amount of time, energy, and resources we believe you would have to commit to see a positive return. The scale ranges from 1 (lowest commitment) to 16 (highest commitment).

1. *Brand placement to add reality to a game*
   Simply say "yes" to a developer/publisher when they ask.

2. *Use the visual imagery of gaming in your advertising*
   Brief your agency to use gaming codes in your next campaign.

3. *Joint promotion*
   Use games or gaming hardware as prizes/giveaways in an on-pack promotion.

4. *Online viral marketing tool*
   Ask your online agency to create a minigame around your product in the hope it will be emailed far and wide as "cool."

5. *Advertising in gaming media*
   Brief your media agency to consider gaming media – magazines, websites, TV shows – as a place for your ads.

6. *Virtual product demos*
   Create a minigame (to sit on your website) that demonstrates your product's difference/superiority.

7. *Gaming event sponsorship*
   Become a sponsor of one of the many and various gaming events going on locally, nationally, and globally.

8. *Sponsor a gaming sports star or team*
   Just like regular sports stars, champion gamers and clans are seeking sponsors with whom to share their winning ways.

9. *Use gaming as an online CRM tool*
   Use gaming to make your website more "sticky": i.e. keep people longer and encourage them to enter their contact details so you can build a powerful CRM database.

10. *Re-segment your audience by gaming typologies*
    Looking for new ways to target people? Think of them as gamers who also buy your product and see new ways to target them, new channels to explore, and new offers to provide.

11. *Gaming character endorsement*
    Endorse a gaming character as a celebrity ambassador for your brand.

12. *In-game advertising*
    Hire a specialist in-game advertising agency to create a campaign and "serve" it in real time to gamers the world over whilst they are playing.

13. *Seed new products in-game*
    Rather than give your latest product to minor celebrities in the hope someone will see them using it, why not get your product used in a new game where you can control its use and be sure it's seen by all who play?

14. *New route to market*
    Target gamers directly – in gaming stores, in the gaming aisle, online, at gaming events, and via peer-to-peer sales. Build a new route to market through the gaming value chain.

15. *In-game commerce*
    Sell your products in games. Dominos can do it with pizza, why shouldn't you be able to do it with your product?

16. *Create your own "Triple A" game*
    Form a joint venture with a developer/publisher and develop a game from scratch. It has to be state of the art or it's not worth it.

Create an opportunity framework

To find the right way forward for leveraging gaming for your brand we strongly suggest creating an opportunity framework. This comes in two parts:

1. *Idea Matrix*
   Starts with consumer insight and helps generate ideas.

2. *Opportunity Matrix*
   Captures each idea and lays it out for evaluation.

In our work with major brand owners we favored the formats shown in Figure 8.6 – although, of course, others would work; it's the principle here that's important.

To use this matrix, first develop a series of insights into your consumers who have some involvement in gaming, and list the associated needs. Then, consider the list of strategic options and try connecting them with the need and your product/service. Finally, capture the ideas and look for gaming properties that fit your brand equities (from the comparison made in the framework set out in Figure 8.5).

Once you have generated a list of ideas, it is worth capturing them in an Opportunity Matrix for easier evaluation. You can tune this to your own business needs. We have developed this example around a multi-national FMCG company with several brands within a given sector (Figure 8.7a).

It is then easy to plot the ideas onto a 2x2 matrix to prioritize them, as in Figure 8.7b.

Conclusion: it's time to play!

If you are considering computer gaming as a way of leveraging your brand, then we hope this book has given you some practical help. Even if you only read it to stump your boss and impress your colleagues, we hope it's given you some food for thought!

Certainly, this will not be the last you hear of the gaming phenomenon. We wrote this book in the belief that we were about to witness a sea change in the way that global media operate. After all, with TV

Figure 8.6

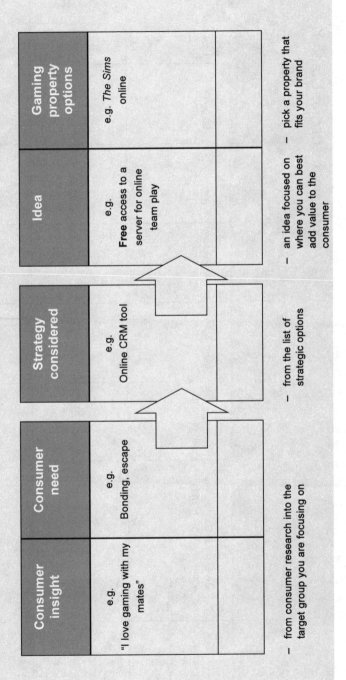

Idea matrix

Consumer insight	Consumer need	Strategy considered	Idea	Gaming property options
e.g. "I love gaming with my mates"	e.g. Bonding, escape	e.g. Online CRM tool	e.g. **Free** access to a server for online team play	e.g. *The Sims* online

– from consumer research into the target group you are focusing on

– from the list of strategic options

– an idea focused on where you can best add value to the consumer

– pick a property that fits your brand

Figure 8.7a

Opportunity matrix for Brand X

Idea	Core target	Passion point	Occasion	Brand	Markets	Equity or volume driver	Size/ reach	Ease/cost
e.g. Free access to a server for online team play of *The Sims*	e.g. 22–30-year-old females who are actively social	e.g. Gaming with my friends	e.g. Evening in with the girls	e.g. Brand X	e.g. USA, Europe	e.g. Equity	e.g. 100,000	e.g. Low cost
Etc.								
Etc								

Figure 8.7b

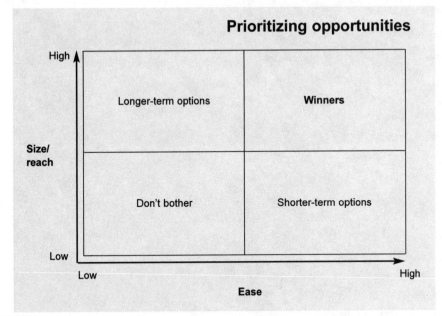

audiences declining, Hollywood movies corpsing at the box office, and the old radio and music industries revolutionized by Internet downloads, it is clear that something is going on out there! And in writing this book, we have all become increasingly convinced that gaming will be at the heart of what comes next, offering brands a new way of reaching out to a truly global audience of all ages, in any place, at any time of the day or night.

Ladies and gentlemen, the future is now fully loaded. ... It's time to play!

CHAPTER 9

Brands and gaming

FAQs

We all know how tough it is to break a new topic in marketing – despite the fact that marketing is supposed to be a hotbed of new ideas! Which is not to say that marketeers aren't open-minded, free-thinking, innovative risk-takers, of course. It's just that any involvement of brands in gaming will almost certainly have to be signed off by people who may be ... what shall we say? ... not quite so close to the cutting edge of contemporary culture.

So if you do find yourself in the position of advocating a gaming strategy to a skeptical finance director or a quizzical CEO, here's a simple way of bringing the key points to life. It may also come in handy as a reference for press calls, team meetings, and briefings. These are our answers to the ten questions that most often come up when discussing the role of gaming as a new marketing asset.

1. Is gaming really that big?

For such a massive global phenomenon, gaming seems easy to miss. It is rarely covered by the news media and sits below the radar of most mainstream advertisers and marketeers. This, despite the fact that our research suggests that in some parts of Europe as many as 83 percent of people play some form of computer or video game on a regular basis. And Europe lags some way behind the world's real gaming hotspots in the Far East, where in countries like South Korea gaming is now the national sport, reported on national TV news right after the main bulletin and before the soccer and basketball scores. Indeed, at its lowest level it's almost as if some people game without realizing they're doing so! If you don't consider yourself a "gamer," ask yourself – have you ever played a quick game of Snake on your mobile phone? Have you ever played Solitaire on your PC? Have you ever helped out a daughter or niece with *The Sims*?

The huge global nature of gaming translates into some pretty impressive figures, too. Gaming has a market value of over $25 billion. That's bigger than the film industry, bigger than the music industry, and even bigger than the home video industry. More striking still is the industry's growth rate. While the other media mentioned are growing slowly, have reached a plateau, or are even in decline, analysts at PricewaterhouseCoopers have projected the worldwide games industry revenue (revenues from hardware, software, and peripherals) to increase from $25.4 billion in 2004 to $54.6 billion in 2009. Which means the games industry is doubling every five years! And the businesses that serve this industry are booming as never before.

PlayStation is now the most successful division of Sony, while the top games publisher Electronic Arts has muscled its way into the list of the *FT*'s Top 500 Global Companies. In fact, gaming has spawned a whole new culture with its own international competitions and megastars, its own language, and its own unique social events and occasions. We believe that gaming has the potential to be as important a marketing medium as radio, cinema, or TV. No, let's take that back. It has the potential to be bigger!

2. Isn't gaming just for teenage boys?

Sure, teenage boys are some of the most enthusiastic gamers around, but that's far from being the whole story. Look at the age profile of Sony PlayStation 2 owners and you can see this straight away: 29.2 percent of PlayStation 2s are used by the 24–34 age group and there is even a significant proportion in the 35+ age bracket. That means half of the user base of the world's most popular games-dedicated console is made up of people over 24 years old – in other words, out of college and already earning. And when you think about it, that would have to be the case; these consoles retail at somewhere between £200 and £300, so it is hardly something that teenagers or students can pick up with their loose change. This is supported by the fact that some of the most popular games, like *Tiger Woods Golf*, *Championship Manager*, and several flight simulators, clearly appeal to mature players. Girls and women are also getting in on the act, wooed by dancemats and female-targeted games like Sony's *SingStar* and Microsoft's *Hearts*; indeed, women now make up 60 percent of players on the ever popular *Sims Online*. And if you don't believe it, just check with one or two of the female PAs in your office about what they were doing on their PCs over lunch!

3. Isn't gaming just for entertainment brands?

Was TV just for technology brands? Is radio just for music brands? We are still right at the beginning of gaming's emergence as a significant media presence, and, of course, it is hard to predict exactly how it will develop. But we believe the situation today is analogous to the position in which marketeers found themselves in the early days of TV. Once again, we are witnessing the birth of a new medium capable of delivering mass audiences, in this case on a global scale. There is absolutely no reason why its appeal should be restricted to entertainment brands – and the mega brands in industries from soft drinks to sportswear, from fast cars to fast food seem to agree. Certainly, many of them are already scrambling to gain a precious first foothold in the gaming arena. And, crucially, it is those brands that enter the gaming arena now that will enjoy a level of kudos and credibility that the later-entry, "me too" brands will find difficult to match.

4. Doesn't gaming only give us opportunities for more presence marketing?

Oh, come on! Use your imagination! Just look at the huge recent growth in "interactive" TV advertising for things like holidays ("Press the red button …"). TV has achieved this with technology that looks positively Jurassic compared to the kit used by the average gamer, so just think what gaming can offer.

Particularly as the number of games going online with multi-player versions increases exponentially, there are more and more opportunities for integrating full web functionality into gaming – with banner ads, click-through counts, sign-ups, the lot! Just take a look at the phenomenally successful Electronic Arts US website pogo.com, a games site sponsored (and paid for) by adverts that pop up periodically during a gaming session. This site already receives more than 14 million unique users every month (70 percent of whom are female, with the majority being over 35) and of course the gamers are already online, so it's just a short step to a sponsor's site with any manner of interactive sales channels at their disposal. What is more, in-game ad agencies are already successfully serving ads in real time to gaming sessions and there is also the potential to use games as a sales channel and a CRM tool. But, of course, that's only just the start of it!

5. Our brand is truly global, so how can gaming be relevant to it?

It is difficult to think of a more global entity than gaming. By its very nature it transcends national, cultural, and linguistic barriers. Just think about it: it is a hugely visual medium, and games are released globally with little or no localization of the software code, so gamers from Beijing to Buenos Aires and from Sydney to Seattle will be playing the same game, enjoying the same experiences at the same time, and often with each other online! Just imagine if you could launch a product globally and reach your entire audience, simultaneously, through just one medium, so that you can not only talk to your target consumers but enable them to experience and interact with your brand. Hmmm ... just imagine!

6. Gaming is only for evening occasions at home, isn't it?

Plenty of people like to come home from work, school, or college and unwind by playing a few computer games. But that is only one of many gaming occasions. For many people, gaming is, above all else, a social activity that will see friends gathering around a PlayStation or Xbox before heading out for the evening, or meeting up in the early hours and playing till dawn, or simply be the destination event itself. Mobile gaming, the fastest-growing area of the industry, throws up all kinds of unpredictable occasions – waiting in reception areas, queuing for tickets, sitting on buses – that have yet to be adequately identified and targeted. It also allows gamers to take their games with them when they go on holiday or on a business trip! The new phenomenon that we call "active gaming" will take gaming into the gym and make it a key health and fitness activity. And, when the rest of the world catches up with the trendsetters of South East Asia, we will see gaming at a LAN arena becoming a central part of a mainstream evening out.

7. Isn't gaming a sedentary pursuit and part of the obesity issue?

To say that gaming is part of the obesity issue is a bit like saying that chairs make you fat. It isn't your armchair that makes you fat; it's the quantity and quality of food that you eat and the kind of lifestyle you pursue. And exactly the same argument applies to games (and TV, cinema, video, listening to music ...). There is absolutely no evidence to suggest that people who game are more likely to be obese. Period.

Indeed, as mentioned above, the emergence of what we call "active gaming" looks set to revolutionize the health and fitness industry, allowing people to exercise at home with *EyeToy*, *Dancemats*, and plug-and-play peripherals such as snowboards. Many of us will soon be enjoying more challenging work-outs in the gym with sophisticated gaming machines like *Cyberfit*, too. So, in future, gaming looks like being anything but a sedentary pursuit.

8. Will gaming replace TV?

This is an interesting one. In our view it will certainly change TV viewing habits dramatically for generation Y: those who are now in their early 20s and younger. And it will certainly be one of the most important factors accelerating the overall decline in traditional TV viewing among other age groups (along with the spread of personal video recorders, multi-channel digital TV, and video on-demand). Quite simply, if, as we know to be the case, the majority of consumers in key categories (particularly in the 10–40 age bracket) are spending an average of 4–5 hours per week playing computer games, then this is 4–5 hours per week that they are not spending doing something else – and TV is one of the major losers here.

For decades, brand owners have relied on the 30-second TV spot as the surest way of reaching a mass audience, so a change in TV viewing habits as significant as this will obviously have a huge effect on how brand owners get their message across. That doesn't mean that TV is likely to go away, but it will no longer be the default way to reach a broad mainstream audience – which means that alternative advertising channels like gaming are certain to become much more important. Basically, if you are not plugged into gaming in the next ten years, you will be missing out on an increasingly large mainstream audience.

9. Doesn't gaming make kids violent?

There is no conclusive evidence to support the idea that the portrayal of violence in games translates into real violence in the playground or on the streets. But, of course, that hasn't stopped critics of gaming from pointing the finger. In fact, their argument is similar to the one that has raged for years over other media: do films make kids violent? Does TV? The jury has been out for a long time on those questions and it will no doubt be out for just as long on the question of violence in gaming as well.

For now, suffice to say that the games industry is regulated in much the same way films are, with certificates suggesting a minimum age for players, but obviously parents themselves have to take responsibility for what their kids do.

In fact, there is also a growing body of evidence that attests to the positive effects of gaming on kids – suggesting that it improves IQ, memory, and co-ordination, among other things – but perhaps that's another story!

10. So, are my competitors getting into gaming?

Yes, almost certainly! Nike, Reebok, Coke, Pepsi, Red Bull, McDonald's, Fiat, and Ford are among the big guns already heavily involved in gaming. And where major brands like these lead, others are bound to follow. The games industry is currently evolving at a frighteningly fast pace and the brands already in the arena are constantly seeking to consolidate their positions with streams of innovative new initiatives.

One good way of keeping up to date with what is going on in this field is to subscribe to the B.I.G. (Brands In Gaming) bulletin, which details these kinds of developments on a monthly basis, as well providing a heads-up to the next big opportunity areas. Subscription details can be found on page 162.

Gaming genres

Third-person action

Typically shooters including an element of adventure and/or puzzling; the gamer's view is of the character they control, often with a choice of angles.

Biggest titles:

Tomb Raider series
Max Payne series
Resident Evil series

Expert view: The perspective affords the gamer a wide-angle view of the action, allowing greater speed and more elaborate effects than would otherwise be possible.

Interesting fact: Tomb Raider's heroine, Lara Croft, is the most recognizable games character of them all, with a recent survey suggesting more people recognized her than recognized either George Bush or Tony Blair!

Active gaming

Games which involve a degree of calorie-burning physical interaction from the gamer in order to control the on-screen action.

Biggest titles:

Dance Dance Revolution Ultramix 2
Tony Hawk's Underground 2
EyeToy: Play 2

Expert view: Originally aimed at younger gamers, this is a sector which is maturing quickly, with the likes of Nike and Reebok now using gaming to target new consumer groups.

Interesting fact: One of the fastest growing gaming sectors, and poised to negate the couch potato image of gamers.

Adventure

Games in which discovery and puzzle solving, usually by using objects found in the local environment, are key. Games in this genre often have a fantasy theme.

Biggest titles:
Final Fantasy series
Alone in the Dark series
Myst series

Expert view: As technology provides ever greater in-game realism, this genre is moving from simple "point-and-click" puzzle solving in front of pre-rendered backdrops to exploration in fully 3D environments.

Interesting fact: The *Final Fantasy* series is one of the most enduring of them all, and is now in its 12th edition; it has also spawned a series of sell-out concerts of the in-game music (composed by Nobuo Uematsu) performed by renowned orchestras such as the Los Angeles Philharmonic.

Beat 'em up

Games of hand-to-hand combat, usually martial arts or wrestling-based, with the emphasis on arcade-style action rather than realism.

Biggest titles:
Tekken series
Soul Calibre series
Def Jam series

Expert view: One of the longest-surviving genres, its days are now numbered due to the technology-driven consumer pull for engaging narrative. Expect to see beat 'em up style action appearing in other genres (particularly third-person action).

Interesting fact: Dance mat-style controllers may give beat 'em ups a new lease of life in the calorie-burning active gaming genre.

Driving – adventure

As the name suggests, games in this genre are a mix of arcade style driving and narrative-driven adventuring.

Biggest titles:
Grand Theft Auto series
The Getaway series
The Italian Job

Expert view: Providing a glimpse of the future of gaming, this category combines two previously separate genres, arcade driving and third-person action, to create a single more immersive and more complete gaming experience.

Interesting fact: *Grand Theft Auto: San Andreas* took more money in its opening weekend than all three *Lord Of The Rings* movies put together took on their opening weekends!

Driving – arcade

High-octane driving, with games typically offering a wide range of supercharged vehicles and a variety of locations, often real world.

Biggest titles:
Gran Turismo series
Need for Speed series
Midnight Club series

Expert view: This category is moving ever closer to the driving-simulation genre with improved graphical and audio realism. It is likely to prosper in its own right, however, thanks to greater levels of user customization and more forgiving physics.

Interesting fact: Published by the world's biggest publisher, Electronic Arts, the *Need For Speed* series is their number two franchise, second only to *FIFA*.

Driving – simulation

Realistic recreations of high end driving/motorcycling experiences, featuring realistic physics, weather conditions, and real-life circuits.

Biggest titles:

Colin McRae Rally series
ToCA Race Driver series
MotoGP series

Expert view: The addition of peripherals, such as steering wheels and pedal sets, has added greatly to the immersion and realism of the experience. This market is set to boom, with a new generation of peripherals such as fold-away racing seats and even racing headsets with built-in microphones.

Interesting fact: Real world professional racing car drivers, such as Bob Earl, use gaming simulations to hone their skills and provide valuable circuit experience.

Flight simulation

Does exactly what it says on the tin. From the sort of aircraft would-be pilots train on at a local airfield to historic icons to the most mighty military aircraft on the planet. Or above it.

Biggest titles:

Microsoft Flight Simulator series
IL-2 Sturmovik series
Ace Combat series

Expert view: Flight sims can often be upgraded with photo-realistic scenery, and feature aircraft accurate in every detail. Indeed, many trainee pilots now use flight sim games to rack-up valuable experience as part of their training for the private pilot's licence (PPL).

Interesting fact: It is now commonplace for many of the world's air forces to use modified military flight sim games to help train their pilots, cutting down greatly on the expense of developing bespoke software.

First-person shooter (FPS)

Games in which the player is the character and is in the game – controlling his or her view of the environment and taking on enemies with a variety of weaponry.

Biggest titles:
Half-Life series
Halo series
Call of Duty series

Expert view: Story-driven narrative will continue to drive the single player aspect, but the mid to long-term future of the genre is online multi-player gaming.

Interesting fact: First-person shooters are the staple diet of the majority of the world's top professional gamers, with some tournaments boasting prize money in excess of $1 million.

Management

Predominantly for the PC, management games allow gamers to both macro and micro-manage realistic simulations of real-world situations such as a theme park or city.

Biggest titles:
RollerCoaster Tycoon series
SimCity series
Theme Hospital

Expert view: Traditionally single-player only and likely to remain so, management titles allow would-be entrepreneurs to practice their skills in financial safety.

Interesting fact: Many management titles are now so realistic that in a recent competition to find the best Sim City player the top prize was complete backing to run as a candidate to becomes London's new mayor!

Massively multi-player online first-person shooter (MMOFPS)

A vast, persistent virtual world in which thousands of gamers are divided into two sides, battling for supremacy. Killed players re-spawn and rejoin the game, and may drop in or out at any time, with the war continuing to rage in their absence.

Biggest title:
Planetside

Expert view: The future of the first-person shooter, these epic games allow players to become emotionally involved with the storyline, and to get to know dozens of other players and game with them regularly.

Interesting fact: Although there is currently only one (PC) game in this genre, the next generation of consoles will ensure this category grows quickly over the next 3–5 years.

Massively multi-player online role-playing game (MMORPG)

Players control a character in a perpetual online world (typically fantasy or futuristic), simultaneously inhabited by upwards of 100,000 other characters controlled by gamers from around the world.

Biggest titles:
World of Warcraft
Ultima Online series
EverQuest series

Expert view: Destined to become a mainstay of mainstream gaming as consoles begin to offer an experience previously available only to PC gamers. Game worlds will become bigger and boast more complex social structures.

Interesting fact: Many gamers make a full-time living buying and selling in-game goods for real world money. Indeed, players of *EverQuest* collectively count for annual gross exports in excess of $6 million, and the game's currency, platinum pieces (PPs), are more valuable than the Japanese yen!

Mobile phones

A variety of downloadable titles, ranging from classic puzzle games to cut-down versions of the latest PC and console titles.

Biggest titles:
Star Wars Episode III: Revenge of the Sith
Military Madness
AMF Xtreme Bowling

Expert view: While technology is ensuring that mobile phone games are rapidly improving both graphically and in complexity of the game mechanics, they are still used predominantly for time-kill and boredom relief and are not considered by gamers to offer true "gaming" experiences.

Interesting fact: Mobile phone games have traditionally been written in the Java programming language but this is increasingly being replaced by the more flexible and more user-friendly language, Brew.

Platform

Usually presented in a cartoon-like world; gamers control a character through a variety of locations, trying to avoid environmental traps whilst collecting points and "power-ups" (objects giving the character an extra one-off, short-term ability).

Biggest titles:
Psychonauts
Rayman series
Mario series

Expert view: One of the oldest genres, originally presented in a side-on 2D view and now increasingly in 3D. The Technicolor worlds and instantly recognizable cartoon-style characters appeal as much to the younger gamer today as ever.

Interesting fact: Two of the best-known game characters of all, Mario and Sonic the Hedgehog, have been awarded stars on San Francisco's Walk of Game (the games industry equivalent of Hollywood's Walk of Fame).

Puzzle

A broad category ranging from traditional board games to tactical puzzle challenges in three dimensions.

Biggest titles:
Tetris series
Bomberman series
Lumines

Expert view: This genre is likely to sub-divide, with the more action-packed titles merging with the third-person action genre, leaving this genre to the board game style titles. It is therefore likely to rapidly decrease in size over next 2–4 years.

Interesting fact: *Minesweeper* is still one of the most frequently played of all PC games, due to three key facts: 1) it is sold with every computer; 2) it is instantly accessible with simple mechanics and rules; 3) it is perfect for killing time.

Real-time strategy (RTS)

Tactical and strategic battles are waged in real time, either as a single player game versus the computer, or increasingly as a multi-player game.

Biggest titles:
Total War series
Star Wars: Empire at War
StarCraft series

Expert view: Technological improvements, particularly in processor speed, are contributing to the complexity of battles, which are increasingly being waged online thanks to the continuing take-up of broadband. The next logical evolutionary step is the birth of the MMORTS (Massively Multi-Player Online Real-Time Strategy) genre!

Interesting fact: *StarCraft* is the most popular game in South Korea, played by millions of people every day, with upwards of 1000 gamers competing against each other in realtime over one of the country's thousands of LANs (Local Area Networks).

Real-time tactics (RTT)

Sister genre to the RTS but requiring more patience and a greater degree of finesse as gamers micro-manage an elite group of fighters.

Biggest titles:
Commandos series
Desperados series

Expert view: RTT titles are usually single player only but are expected to follow the logical progression to multi-player Internet gaming.

Interesting fact: An interesting example of a genre sub-dividing as it grows, RTT titles were originally bundled in the RTS category, but the genre is now well-established in its own right.

Role-playing game (RPG)

Usually set in fantasy or futuristic locations, players control a character through an adventure littered with battles and intrigue. The use of magic is usually crucial.

Biggest titles:

Baldur's Gate series
Guild Wars
Dungeon Siege series

Expert view: One of the most engaging genres as players control a character, or avatar, they have created from a preset palette of variables to determine attributes such as strength, dexterity, skill with magic, and the like.

Interesting fact: This genre stems from the classic dice-based Dungeons and Dragons games.

Simulation

As the name suggests, games in this category provide simulations, often obsessive in their realism, of anything from a variety of vehicles to virtual people.

Biggest titles:

The Sims series
Mobile Train Simulator
Freelancer

Expert view: Once considered a niche genre, and definitely just for the PC, simulations are enjoying something of a renaissance across all platforms thanks largely to the phenomenally successful *The Sims* series.

Interesting fact: *The Sims* is the biggest selling franchise for the PC, with female gamers accounting for approximately 60 percent of all players.

Sports – arcade

Sports titles in which realism takes a back seat to fun and in which extra moves can often be "unlocked" by reaching certain goals within the game.

Biggest titles:
Tony Hawk's series
SSX series
Backyard Skateboarding 2006

Expert view: A dominant and particularly "cool" genre that is beginning to attract sports simulation titles to exploit its edgy feel (e.g. *FIFA Street*).

Interesting fact: Peripherals are allowing gamers to practice real-world sporting skills in the comfort of their living rooms – without hindrance from the weather or risk of injuries.

Sports – management

A genre that allows gamers to take control of their favorite clubs etc. and guide them to glory as their manager or coach.

Biggest titles:
Championship Manager series
Football Manager series
Pro Rugby Manager series

Expert view: Traditionally the preserve of the PC due to the games' need for number crunching, these enduringly popular games are set to increase their presence in the gaming world as the next-gen consoles get in on the act.

Interesting fact: These games have been enormously successful despite the fact that until this year they have been completely text based, featuring no graphics at all!

Sports – simulation

Gamers control the on-screen players of a sports team; often played as a two or four-player game.

Biggest titles:
FIFA series
Madden NFL series
NHL series

Expert view: The most popular of all the sports genres, and now included in the World Cyber Games (annual gaming "Olympics") through the inclusion of the FIFA titles.

Interesting fact: The FIFA series is the biggest franchise of Electronic Arts (the world's largest publisher), with more than 50 million units sold to date.

Stealth

Viewed in either first or third-person perspective, these games place the emphasis firmly on clandestine approaches to missions and achieving goals with the minimum of disturbance.

Biggest titles:
Thief series
Metal Gear series
Splinter Cell series

Expert view: Delivering on the consumer pull for gamers to be allowed to play games their way, this genre targets all those gamers who enjoy a patient build-up and detailed planning as much as actioning an event.

Interesting fact: The Splinter Cell series has been developed in conjunction with best-selling author Tom Clancy, who has founded his own game development company, Red Storm Entertainment.

Turn-based strategy

Strategy titles in this genre differ from their RTS cousins in that time pressures (if any) are presented only by a clock, and not by their opponents amassing forces!

Biggest titles:

Civilization series
Worms series
Risk

Expert view: This genre now feels very outdated thanks to strategy games in real-time (RTS) and is fast becoming redundant, though it may yet be thrown a lifeline (see below).

Interesting fact: Mobile phone games are likely to pick up this genre as their limitations in data transfer speeds preclude offering the RTS, while turn-based strategy presents no such problems.

Main games publishers

Platform owners

Microsoft
Sony
Nintendo

First-tier games publishers

North America
Acclaim Entertainment
Activision, Inc.
Electronic Arts
THQ
Take-Two Interactive

Europe
Codemasters
Eidos
Infogrames Entertainment
Ubisoft
Vivendi

Japan
Atari
Sega

Second-tier games publishers

Buena Vista Games
Capcom
Fox Interactive
Hasbro Interactive
Konami
LucasArts Entertainment Company
Majesco
Midas Interactive
Midway Games Ltd
Namco
Sammy
SCi Entertainment Group PLC
Sold Out Software
Square Enix
Taito

Glossary of gaming terms

First of all, essential gamer's slang

The slang	The translation
AFAICS, AFAIK, AFAIR	(*As Far As I Can See/Know/Recall*) To the best of my knowledge
AIUI	(*As I Understand It*) See above
ATM	(*At The Moment*) For now
BRB	(*Be Right Back*) Indicates user is taking a short break – usually refreshment/comfort!
BTW	(*By The Way*) No explanation needed
BYOC	(*Bring Your Own Computer*) Used for MMP festivals/tournaments where players bring their own equipment
FOAD	(*F*** Off And Die*) Pretty self-explanatory really
G1	(*Good One*) Can mean either "Well done" or "Good joke." *See also* "N1"
GG	(*Good Game*) Usually posted at the end of an online team/individual game
HAND	(*Have A Nice Day*) Can be genuinely meant, but often used ironically
HTH	(*Hope This Helps*) Often added at the end of an email or newsgroup post answering a question

IANAL	(*I Am Not A Lawyer*). Popular ironic term meaning "Don't ask me"/"how should I know?"
IIRC	(*If I Recall Correctly*) No explanation needed
IMO, IMHO	(*In My (Honest) Opinion*) No explanation needed
ISTM	(*It Seems To Me*) No explanation needed
ISTR	(*I Seem To Recall*) No explanation needed
LMAO	(*Laughing My Ass Off*) Very funny; the equivalent of an emoticon
LOL	(*Laughing Out Loud*) Even funnier
LOM	(*Low On Manna*) A term used in RPGs where "manna" is a general property required for the execution of spells etc.
MP	(*My Pleasure*) Speaks for itself
N1	(*Nice One*) Can mean either "Well done" or "Good joke." *See also* "G1'
Newbie	(*New beginner*) Internet slang for someone who hasn't been using computers or the Internet long
Off-topic	A message which is not relevant to a particular newsgroup or forum on the Internet is said to be "off-topic;" posting off-topic messages in newsgroups annoys people intensely, as they make it harder to follow the discussion properly
OMFG	(*Oh My F****** God!*) General exclamation of surprise/shock
ROFL (or ROTFL)	(*Rolling On the Floor Laughing*) Can it get much funnier?
ROFLMAO	(*Rolling On the Floor Laughing My Ass Off*) Evidently it can!
RTFM	(*Read The F****** Manual*) Internet slang, usually fired at people asking basic questions to which they would know the answers if they had looked at the manual

TY	(*Thank You*) Speaks for itself, really
TYVM	(*Thank You Very Much*) As above
WTF?	(*What The F***?*) General exclamation of surprise/shock, or simply a question
WTG	(*Way To Go*) "Well played;" usually posted at the end of a game where a winner is publicly declared
WYSIWYG	(*What You See Is What You Get*; pr. "whizzy-wig") A reference to very straightforward gaming mechanics or to the writer, meaning they are not pretending to be something they're not
YMMV	(*Your Mileage May Vary*) "Your experience may be different;" derives from a disclaimer in US car ads
YW/YVW	(*You're (Very) Welcome*) No explanation needed

Second, everything you ever wanted to know about gaming but were afraid to ask! And then some ...

The code	*The translation*
80211a, 80211b, 80211g, 80211i	Different standards for operating wireless networks (wi-fi). Loosely the higher the letter, the faster the speed. So far they are mostly incompatible with each other.
AGP	(*Advanced Graphics Port*) A slot on the PC motherboard for the latest generation of graphics cards, and the format of the cards themselves. Standard on new PCs from 1998. "AGP x 2" runs at twice the speed of the original AGP.
AI	(*Artificial Intelligence*) A program designed to respond "intelligently" to various situations, for example the computer opponent(s) in a game.
Always-on	An Internet connection which remains on 24/7 such as ADSL or cable, rather than only connecting on demand like a dialup. The only sort online gamers use.

Avatar	An in-game character or persona controlled by the gamer, and often created by them using in-game character construction options, e.g. gender, hair color, clothing.
Backwards-compatible	A program (or system) designed to work with data generated by earlier versions of itself, even though the format may since have changed completely. Games platforms need to be backwards compatible in order for gamers to be able to continue playing their favorite games when they buy the latest generation console. Nintendo hope to steal a march with their next-gen console, "Revolution," through making their entire back catalog of games across all their previous platforms available free of charge online.
Beat 'em up	A computer game in which you control one or more characters fighting onscreen using karate, kung-fu, wrestling, and so forth.
Bit	The smallest unit of information in a computer (equals 0 or 1); eight bits equal one byte.
Blog	(*weBLOG*) A website documenting someone's life and/or thoughts. Very popular among the MMORPG communities, where gamers often choose to write diaries as their avatars describing their day-to-day experiences in the game world.
Bluetooth	A wireless communication system for PCs and other computing devices. Bluetooth devices from different manufacturers won't always communicate with each other reliably, and the system is now under threat from faster wireless technologies (*see* wi-fi).
Bps	(*Bits Per Second*) A measure of how quickly infor mation is being transferred, usually via a modem or network; high transfer rates are essential for online play.
Brew	(*Binary Runtime Environment for Wireless*) Not an operating system, but an environment in which applications run; it is used for creating mobile

phone games and is a more sophisticated protocol than Java.

Broadband   Internet access over a connection much faster than an ordinary modem.

Bug   Error, especially in a program, that has been missed in quality assurance (games testing). Legend has it that an insect got inside one of the original (and huge) computers, where it was unceremoniously cremated causing a system failure (the computer that is, not the bug. Well, that too). Games are increasingly getting better at being shipped bug-free, though it is still commonplace for PC games to be shipped with some errant programming which is then fixed through additional "patches" of code (*see* patch).

Byte   A basic unit of measurement for pieces of information; the space required to store one character (see also bit, kilobyte, megabyte, gigabyte, terabyte).

CD-ROM, CD-R   (*Compact Disc-Read Only Memory*) A misnomer, as strictly speaking it is not memory but storage. Physically identical to standard music CDs. Currently the most popular medium on which to burn programs, as it can hold literally hundreds of times as much information as a standard floppy disk, about 650 megabytes in total. Once a CD-ROM has been created its contents cannot be changed. Starting to be replaced by DVD (Digital Versatile Disc) for games since they now contain far too much data to be stored on even several CDs.

Cable   An always-on high-speed Internet connection similar to ADSL but capable of higher speeds, which uses cable TV technology instead of a phone line.

Character   An in-game persona, such as Mario or Lara – with the corresponding branding opportunities. Also, a letter of the alphabet, number, space, or punctuation mark.

Compression   A way of making files smaller, either to fit into restricted storage space or to speed up transmission over the Internet. Popular compression standards include JPEG and GIF for pictures, MP3 for music files, and zip for just about everything else. It is an advanced form of this technology, "Steam," which heralds the new format for games distribution (*see also* Steam).

Console
A dedicated gaming platform such as the Play-Station 3, Xbox 360, or Revolution. Originally meant a terminal connected to a mainframe computer.

Crack, cracked
A crack is a small program intended to defeat software's copy protection, thus allowing unlicensed copies to be made – stealing it, in effect. Software which is distributed with its copy protection disabled or bypassed has been "cracked." As you might imagine, games software offers a sizeable opportunity for unscrupulous "crackers."

DDR
(*Double Data Rate*) A very fast type of RAM for a PC, originally only used on high-performance graphics cards but now being used for general memory in most high-end PCs. Hugely preferable, if not essential, for high-spec, processor-hungry games.

Disk
Generic term for a type of storage device, such as a hard disk or a floppy disk (diskette). So called because the important part, where the information is actually stored, is circular, although on a floppy you can't see it because it is hidden away inside a protective shell.

Driver
A small program used by the operating system to control hardware such as a sound or video card. Often downloading the latest driver for a device from the manufacturer's website will improve its functionality, thus improving the gameplay experience, and perhaps giving the user a competitive edge.

DVD
(Digital Versatile Disc) A more advanced version of the standard CD which can hold far more information, DVD readers and writers are now standard on most new PCs.

E-commerce
Conducting business over the Internet, particularly

	the World Wide Web. This is now used widely by gamers for the trading of in-game characters, equipment, skills etc.
Emoticon	(*EMOTion ICON*) A group of symbols used to indicate emotions in emails, newsgroups, forums etc., and particularly popular with non-hardcore gamers, who prefer acronyms and other shorthand groups of initials (see slang). The most popular is the smiley:-) or :) (look at it sideways), but there are lots of variations including the sad face :-(, the wink ;-), and the astonished face :-0.
Encrypt/ Encryption	Coding data so that it can't be read by hackers etc. when transmitted over the Internet. For example, any reputable website allowing the purchase of consumer goods (e.g. games, subscriptions for MMORPGs etc.) by credit card will encrypt your credit card number and personal details.
Ethernet	The most popular system used to connect a computer to a network, including most broadband Internet connections. The computer needs to be fitted with a suitable expansion card, usually called an Ethernet card.
Expansion card (or board)	A circuitboard that can be inserted into an expansion slot on the PC's motherboard, to give the PC extra capabilities. Common examples are sound cards, graphics cards (essential for gaming) and network cards.
Expansion slot	A socket on a PC motherboard into which you can insert expansion cards to increase the PC's capabilities. Most PCs have several PCI slots, plus an AGP slot for a graphics card.
Eye candy	Visually stunning game; often used to mean one with superb graphics at the expense of great gameplay.
FAQ	(*Frequently Asked Questions*) A document on a website or in a newsgroup which gives answers to common problems and questions, such as why one cannot get a game to run, or common gameplay tips.

File server	A type of computer used on networks to provide files and other services to other computers. Often just called a server. Used to "run" online multi-player games.
Firewall	Originally a dedicated computer between you and the Internet, preventing hackers, spammers, and similar undesirables from taking over your PC. Now often just an ever-present program running in the background on a PC. Absolutely essential if you have an always-on Internet connection such as ADSL or cable – which is, of course, de rigueur for serious gamers.
Firewire	A standard for very fast data transfer, popular for applications that use very large files, e.g. video editing, in-game cut-scenes. Requires special hardware, generally added to a computer as an expansion card.
Flame	Internet slang for an email or newsgroup post insulting or telling someone off. They range from elegant rapier wit to obscene profanity. Often dependent on gaming genre!
Flamewar	A public trading of insults in a game. All's fair in love and flamewars.
Forum	A public or semi-public area on a website or bulletin board where you can read and post messages on a particular topic, allowing public debate. There are thousands dedicated to gaming, either in general, or more popularly specific to a particular game or platform.
FPS	(*First-Person Shooter*) A computer game where you shoot things (hence the name, natch), played from a first-person perspective, i.e. with you standing behind the gun(s) so as to be a character actually "in" the environment.
Frag	To shoot someone in a computer game, usually a FPS.
GHz	(*Gigahertz*) Billions of cycles per second. Often used as a measurement of a PC processor chip's speed

and power, with bigger numbers meaning a higher speed, and price. 1000 MHz = 1.0 GigaHertz. The more powerful the processor, the faster it can play sophisticated games (see also MHz).

Gigabyte (or Gig)   Unit of measurement for pieces of information: approximately 1 billion bytes, 1 million kilobytes, or 1000 megabytes. Hard disk sizes are usually measured in gigabytes. Often shortened to "GB," "Gig," or just G. Some games now require upwards of 5 GB storage space, and this is expected to double over the next three to five years.

Graphics   A catch-all term for anything involving drawing images on a PC screen. A game with great graphics is one that is visually spectacular (see also eye candy).

Graphics card (or controller)   An expansion card that the PC uses to control the monitor's graphics. Modern PCs have a dedicated slot for graphics cards called AGP, but you can also still get PCI format cards.

Griefer   Someone who deliberately kills members of his/her own team (almost always against the rules, causing extreme annoyance, and gamers who persist in "griefing" are usually suspended or banned from playing).

GUI   (*Graphical User Interface*; pr. "gooey") A program's controls are represented pictorially, with symbols, buttons, and so forth, and mostly controlled by pointing and clicking with a mouse rather than having to type in text commands. Almost all modern software is GUI controlled.

Hacker   Person who uses computers to break into ("hack") systems to which they are not supposed to have access in order to steal, manipulate, or plant information. Famously, the source code for the most popular FPS, *Half-Life 2*, was stolen by hackers, resulting in the game's release being delayed by a year.

Hardware   The physical parts of a computer.

Hotspot   A location in which a computer can connect to a wireless network (see wi-fi).

Hub

A basic device for connecting computers together to form a network.

Intranet

A private miniature Internet that often allows only limited access to the Internet proper. Intranets are useful for allowing easy sharing of confidential files within a clan or guild etc.

IP

(*Internet Protocol*) A protocol (computer language) which computers use to communicate with and over the Internet.

IP address

(*Internet Protocol* address) A unique number assigned to any computer connected to the Internet (including yours!) in the format 255.255.255.255. Each of the four blocks of numbers can be any value from 0 to 255. They can either be assigned permanently ("static IP") or per session ("dynamic IP"). Most ISPs assign them dynamically, i.e. when you connect to the Internet, but a notable example of static IPs are games servers; most serious online gamers will have a note of all their favorite servers in this format to allow quick and easy connection for a gaming session (usually stored in an in-game "favorites" folder).

ISA

(*Industry Standard Architecture*; pr. "icer") A once-common type of PC expansion card, now obsolete (*see also* PCI).

ISP

(*Internet Service Provider*) A company that provides Internet services or a connection to the Internet.

Java

A programming language used to create small programs called applets, often to produce special effects on web pages, and the most common programming language for mobile phone games (*see also* Brew).

JPEG, jpg

(*Joint Picture [Experts] Group*; pr. "jay-peg") A standard type of compressed graphics file, widely used on the WWW. Particularly good for photographs, and the most common format for capturing screenshots of a game to upload to the web for sharing (*see also* compression).

Killer app	(*Killer application*) A program that is so obviously and enormously useful to someone that they will rush out and buy it immediately - and sometimes even a more powerful computer on which to run it! Much anticipated games sometimes acquire this moniker pre-release.
Kbps	(*KiloBits Per Second*) A measure of speed of information flow, usually over a modem. A Kilobit is 1000 bits (*see also* bps, Mbps).
Kilobyte	Unit of measurement for pieces of information: actually 1024 bytes (characters), but in practice almost always rounded down to 1000. Often written as just K, e.g. 250 K is 250 kilobytes (250,000 bytes/ characters – well not exactly, but close enough) (*see also* megabyte, gigabyte).
LAN	(*Local Area Network*; pr. "lan") A network of computers connected together, usually in a single physical space. The great advantage of playing games over a LAN is the total absence of any lag (see below); all major tournaments and practice sessions for clans are run over LANs (*see also* WAN).
Lag	The time gap between data being uploaded from a computer to a server and data from the server being received (called the "ping" time). In practical terms it can mean the difference between shooting an adversary and firing a shot only to discover they had moved before you fired (and probably shot you!) (*see also* ping).
Mac	The Apple Corporation's alternative to the PC, much loved by its devotees but largely incompatible with PCs, though some popular software is also released in Mac format.
Mbps	(*MegaBits Per Second*) A measure of speed of information flow over a network (and if it's measured in Mbps, it's reasonably quick). A Megabit is one million bits (*see also* bps, Kbps).
Megabyte	Unit of measurement for pieces of information:

approximately 1 million bytes or 1000 kilobytes. Often shortened to Meg or just M (*see also* gigabyte, kilobyte, byte).

MegaHertz | *See* MHz.

MHz | (*Megahertz*) Millions of cycles per second. Most often used as a measurement of a PC processor chip's speed and power, with bigger numbers meaning more speed and a higher price (*see also* GHz).

Modem | (*MOdulator/DEModulator*) A device for allowing computers to communicate over a phone line. May be either an expansion card or an external device plugged into one of the serial ports.

Monitor | A PC's screen.

Motherboard | The main circuitboard in the computer, into which all the other bits and pieces are plugged.

Mouse | A device used to move a pointer around on the computer screen. Essential to get the most out of Windows, though it is not quite impossible to use Windows without one. It is impossible to play most PC games though!

Network | A way of linking several computers together so that their users can share resources such as printers and documents, often via a central computer called a server (*see also* LAN, WAN, Ethernet).

Network card, Network Interface Card | An expansion card that lets a PC communicate with a network; required for broadband Internet access (*see also* Ethernet).

Newbie | (*New Beginner*) Gaming slang for someone who is new to a particular game. Online servers will often run several games particularly for newbies so that they can cut their teeth without constantly being annihilated. Often used as a derogatory term for a less able player.

NIC | See Network card.

Off-topic | *See under* Gamer's slang.

Online	Connected to the Internet.
Packet loss	Data lost in upload/download. Data is packaged and sent in small parcels (packets).
Patch	A program that makes updates to computer software, usually to fix bugs that had not been detected when the software went on sale.
PC	(*Personal Computer*) Originally just short for "personal computer," PC is now an industry standard, partly evolved in the marketplace, partly agreed by a committee of the major players in the computer industry.
PCI	(*Peripheral Component Interconnect*) A standard for PC expansion cards, and currently the most popular.
PDF	(*Portable Document Format*) A popular document format, used mainly for online computer manuals, which retains the look of a printed book onscreen. PDFs are created using Adobe Acrobat, but can be read and displayed by many different programs, including Internet Explorer. Games re-released as budget titles usually provide the instructions in this format.
Peripheral	Anything that plugs into the computer, such as keyboard, printer, *EyeToy*, snowboard, dancemat, etc.
Ping	The length of time (measured in milliseconds) it takes for data to upload to/download from a server. The lower the ping time the shorter the delay – and the better the playing experience.
Plug'n'play	(*Plug and Play*) Any device that needs only to plugged in to be ready to use.
Port	A socket on the back (usually) of a computer or console that allows you to plug in extra hardware such as a steering wheel or joystick.
Processor	The nerve center of PCs and consoles: everything flows through it. Also called the CPU. The best known are Intel's Pentium and AMD's Athlon. The

	most important single specification on any PC is the speed of its processor, usually measured in megahertz (MHz), or gigahertz (GHz).
PS2/PS3	Sony's PlayStation 2 games console, and its successor the PlayStation 3.
QA	(*Quality Assurance*) The technical name for play-testing, in which a group of paid (usually poorly) gamers play through a game endlessly, searching for those moments in which it goes awry, then reporting the bug to the programmers who write new code to overcome the problem.
RPG	(*Role-Playing Game*) A genre in which the player controls a character (avatar) and interacts with other characters, explores virtual worlds, undertakes quests etc., often involving swords and sorcery.
RTS	(*Real-Time Strategy*) A genre in which the player commands armies (usually) of animated figures and directs their development. Progress and increases in skill levels often require resource-gathering, the building of a base, researching new technologies etc. The heart and soul of these games is the battles that are waged between the player's forces and those of their opponent(s), either AI or controlled by other players online.
Server	A computer at the center of most networks, which provides files and other services to other computers. Also known as a file server. The hub of all online gaming.
Shockwave	Technology from Macromedia Inc for making games, animations, special effects etc. on a webpage.
Shoot 'em up	Old generic name for first/third-person, and sideways-scrolling, shooters.
Software	The programs that run on a computer. In gaming terms, the games themselves.

Soundcard	An expansion card that enables the PC to make realistic, life-like sounds. Almost all modern PCs are fitted with soundcards; nowadays they are often built into the motherboard instead of being added as an expansion card, though a top-end plug-in soundcard will improve the playing experience of most games no end.
Steam	The brand name for Valve Software's proprietary technology, which allows vast quantities of data to be compressed and then transferred over the Internet – the future of game purchase and delivery.
Terabyte	Unit of measurement for pieces of information: approximately 1 trillion bytes, 1 billion kilobytes, 1 million megabytes or 1000 gigabytes.
TIFF, Tif	(*Tagged Image File Format*) A type of graphics file, used for screenshots when quality is paramount. The files are usually huge, as the data is not significantly compressed. Files in this format usually have names ending .tif.
USB	(*Universal Serial Bus*) A type of serial port (or connector), used to attach extra devices such as a joypad or external soundcard to a PC. USB 2.0 is a faster version of the same thing. Many PCs now use USB to connect the mouse and keyboard.
VGA	(*Video Graphics Array*) An early color-graphics standard for PCs, now used as a sort of lowest common denominator which all monitors and graphics cards understand.
VOIP	(*Voice Over Internet Protocol*) A system by which gamers can communicate with each other in real time simply by speaking, rather than needing to type. The advantages for the speed at which orders/requests can be given are obvious. Also used for making cheap phonecalls over the Internet instead of via the telephone.
WAN	(*Wide Area Network*) A group of networks, or more properly LANs, connected together.

Weblog	A website documenting someone's life and/or thoughts, also known as a blog.
Wi-fi	(*WIreless FIdelity*) A method of connecting computers together in a network without cables, using small transmitter/receivers connected to ordinary PCs, printers, broadband modems etc. (*see also* 80211 etc.).
Winzip	The most popular program for compressing files, either for storage or transmission via the Internet, widely available as a free download. The compressed files it creates have the extension .zip (*see also* zip).
Wireless network	A computer network that uses radio transmitters (usually) to move information between computers without the need for physical cables (*see* wi-fi).
Zip	A popular standard for file compression developed by the PKWare corporation. Files thus compressed usually have the extension .zip (*see* Winzip).

Author biographies

David Nichols

Global Client Director, Added Value

David has a first-class degree in Aerospace engineering from Bristol University, which led him, via postgraduate work designing advanced simulation systems for British Aerospace, into his first job at Ford Motor Company. After two years as a strategy consultant with OC&C, David yearned for something more creative and consumer driven, and joined Added Value – then a budding 35-person marketing consultancy in Hampton Wick.

He has now been at Added Value for 11 fun-filled years, which have seen him spend six months working in Paris before undertaking his first management role: leading the Australian office and, of course, watching the 2000 Olympics in Sydney.

When the company became part of WPP, David took over as Managing Director in the UK, where he was instrumental in developing proprietary methodologies, leading client development and overseeing the recent merger with two other WPP consulting companies.

David specializes in the ideas side of brand strategy: brand positioning, new brand creation, and innovation. He has led projects for major global brands in ice cream, confectionery, pet food, mobile telecommunications, automotive, Internet services, television, laundry, soft drinks, wine, beer, spirits, and computer gaming.

In his current role within the much larger global company, David is responsible for three of the business's largest global clients.

David has written three musicals, one of which, *Flush!*, was optioned by a major producer for a national tour and West End run (but still lies languishing on his desk!). He managed a professional improvization troupe, *The Impro Musical*, for two years working with Eddie Izzard, Tony Slattery, and Tony Hawks.

David is also a keen flyer. In the air he is training to be an aerobatic pilot, and on-line, he revels in being a WWII Spitfire ace in *Combat Flight Simulator*.

David is married to Clare, also a marketing consultant, and they have two delightful daughters, Holly and Imogen.

Tom Farrand

Director, Added Value UK

Born and brought up in East Africa, Tom originally intended to become a zoologist, studying animal behavior. A slight change in direction saw him graduating with a Master's in Biochemistry from Oxford to join Procter & Gamble, working in technical brand management.

Tom spent the formative years of his career in between P&G global technical centers, French beauty salons, American malls, and Japanese bathrooms, getting to grips with people's desires in the world of health and beauty. Working closely with R&D and brand management teams, he focused on translating those insights into new products, claims, and technologies for the Olay and Safeguard brands.

Tom left P&G for an entrepreneurial stint with the team starting up the London office for Differ – a Swedish brand-innovation consultancy working for mobile and Internet-based ventures with Swedish clients such as Ericsson, Telia, and SEB.

In 2001 Tom joined Added Value, where he has worked on a variety of international projects, specializing in innovation, brand stretch, and organizational engagement issues. His clients have included Blockbuster, Lever Faberge, Fritolay, Vodafone, Egg, General Motors, Ford, the Coca-Cola Company, Nestlé, and Beverage Partners Worldwide. He is currently responsible for developing the Added Value global innovation offer and capability within the business.

A keen sportsman, Tom has recently retired from playing rugby and has turned his attention to the "safer" worlds of windsurfing, kitesurfing, and snowboarding. He lives near Wandsworth Common with his wife Gemma and a trusted PlayStation 2 and wired-up gaming PC!

Tom Rowley

Associate Director with Added Value UK
Tom joined Added Value in 1997, following stints in journalism and the music industry. His work at Added Value focuses on applying cultural insight (leading edge/expert insight, trends and semiotics) to diverse brand challenges. Tom has led cultural insight projects across a variety of categories for clients who include Levi's, Bacardi-Martini, and Sainsbury's. He is fluent in French and Italian and has led insight projects in both markets.

Matt Avery

Managing Director, B.I.G.
After graduating with honors from Leeds University, Matt worked as a professional actor and director, working on several Andrew Lloyd Webber productions. He then co-wrote and directed *Flush! The Musical* (set in 1950s America's only unisex public toilet!), which ran for seven months, in three countries, and was optioned for a West End run. At which point he decided to get a proper job. Marketing beckoned, via copywriting, while a long-held passion for computer gaming gave rise to employment as a freelance journalist with best-selling gaming magazines *PC Gamer* and *PC Format*, for whom he still writes occasional features when time allows.

Drama was never far away (in every sense), and in 1999 Matt co-wrote another musical, *Between Love & Passion*, which he co-produced off-West End. He is currently heavily involved in the amateur drama scene as an actor, and tones his strategic muscles playing chess in a non-virtual league in southern England, and in a variety of real-time strategy games online. He also manages two soccer clubs, his local team Southampton and Italian giant Juventus (in *Championship Manager*), runs a very successful theme park (in *RollerCoaster Tycoon 3*) and can regularly be found online playing *Counter-Strike* and *Return To Castle Wolfenstein* (if you ever meet "B.I.G." online you'll know who you're killing!).

In 2003 Matt combined his passions and founded B.I.G. – Brands In Gaming – a unique marketing consultancy that develops strategies for major brand owners to interface with computer gaming and computer gamers. He is currently the Managing Director of this fast-growing business.

Added Value

Added Value is a global marketing insight company that helps clients ignite desire for their brands, businesses, and people by going beyond the obvious. From across our new global network we draw on deep expertise of brand marketing, consumer insight, innovation, and communications optimization to help us provide better answers to the marketing questions our clients are facing today. We take our clients on an invigorating journey to challenge, stretch, and build their thinking to deliver a powerful, actionable, and compelling marketing and communications strategy based on unique consumer insights. We have 21 offices across 13 locations worldwide. Our client list is extensive and includes global brands such as Colgate Palmolive, Vodafone, SAB Miller, General Motors, Harley Davidson, Expedia.com and Campbell's.

For more information visit www.added-value.com or call us on +44 (0) 208 614 1500.

B.I.G. (Brands In Gaming)

Brands In Gaming is a unique marketing consultancy that helps consumer brands develop strategies to leverage computer gaming. With ten years' experience and deep expertise in the games industry as journalists, publishers, and consultants, B.I.G. is leading the charge into the fastest growing entertainment medium on the planet. Founded in 2003 and based in southern England, B.I.G. works across the globe consulting to a number of major blue-chip clients such as Coca-Cola, Vodafone, and Camelot.

B.I.G. also produces monthly bulletins detailing all the latest innovations and opportunities from the world of gaming. Tailored to clients' individual needs, these range from straightforward news-led heads-up on the latest trends, future hardware and software, major brands entering the gaming space, etc., to bespoke, individual, client-focused bulletins on the opportunities and implications the very latest the world of gaming affords for brands, together with recommendations on which assets to leverage to maximize the potential of the opportunity, which deals to broker and with whom (which we can also help clients with), competitor activity in gaming, etc, etc.

For more information visit www.brandsingaming.com, call us on +44 (0) 23 8076 6177 or email us at info@brandsingaming.com.

Acronyms

AR	augmented reality
ARG	augmented-reality gaming
CEO	chief executive officer
CRM	customer relationship management
DJ	disk jockey
DS	dual screen
EA	Electronic Arts
ESA	Entertainment Software Association
FAQs	frequently asked questions
FIFA	Fédération Internationale de Football Association
FMCG	fast-moving consumer goods
FPS	first-person shooter
GPS	global positioning system
IP	intellectual property
KL	Kuala Lumpur
KPI	key performance indicator
LA	Los Angeles
LAN	local area network
MMOFPS	massively multi-player online first-person shooter
MMORPG	massively multi-player online role-playing game
MMORTS	massively multi-player online real-time strategy
MP3	media player 3
MRI	magnetic resonance imaging
PC	personal computer
PDA	personal digital assistant
PR	public relations
PSP	PlayStation Portable

PVR	personal video recorder
RPG	role-playing game
RTS	real-time strategy
RTT	real-time tactics
WCG	World Cyber Games

Index